History and Myth
Postcolonial Dimensions

Edited by

Arti Nirmal
Banaras Hindu University, India

and

Sayan Dey
Wits Centre for Diversity Studies,
University of Witwatersrand, Johannesburg

Series in World History

VERNON PRESS

Copyright © 2022 by the authors.

All rights reserved. No part of this publication may be reproduced, stored in a retrieval system, or transmitted in any form or by any means, electronic, mechanical, photocopying, recording, or otherwise, without the prior permission of Vernon Art and Science Inc.

www.vernonpress.com

In the Americas:
Vernon Press
1000 N West Street, Suite 1200
Wilmington, Delaware, 19801
United States

In the rest of the world:
Vernon Press
C/Sancti Espiritu 17,
Malaga, 29006
Spain

Series in World History

Library of Congress Control Number: 2020946413

ISBN: 978-1-64889-448-0

Also available: 978-1-62273-854-0 [Hardback]; 978-1-64889-340-7 [PDF, E-Book]

Product and company names mentioned in this work are the trademarks of their respective owners. While every care has been taken in preparing this work, neither the authors nor Vernon Art and Science Inc. may be held responsible for any loss or damage caused or alleged to be caused directly or indirectly by the information contained in it.

Every effort has been made to trace all copyright holders, but if any have been inadvertently overlooked the publisher will be pleased to include any necessary credits in any subsequent reprint or edition.

Cover design by Vernon Press. Image by Pexels from Pixabay.

Contents

	Preface	v
	Foreword Diana J. Fox Bridgewater State University, Massachusetts	xi
	Introduction - Decolonization and its Discontents: Democratization, Demarcations, Dangers Waseem Anwar Forman Christian College, Lahore	xvii
	Part I Postcolonialism and/ in Texts: Histories and Myths	1
Chapter 1	**Material Development and Human Regression: A Decolonial Reading of Orijit Sen's *River of Stories*** Diptarup Ghosh Dastidar Amity University, Raipur	3
Chapter 2	**A Tale of Things: Decoloniality of Memory in Orhan Pamuk's *The Museum of Innocence*** Chand Basha M Department of Studies and Research in English, VSK University, Bellary	19
Chapter 3	**Post-9/11, Cultural Amnesia and Representation(s) of Islamophobia in Ayad Akhtar's *Disgraced*** Abhisek Ghosal Ph.D. Research Scholar, Department of Humanities and Social Sciences, Indian Institute of Technology, Kharagpur	35
Chapter 4	**Ancient Stories, Current Praxes: Decolonial Myths in Contemporary Literature** Feroza Jussawalla Professor Emerita of English, University of New Mexico	47

Part II Decoloniality: Experiences and Engagements — 63

Chapter 5 **White as Paper, Black as Ink: Bilali Muhammad and the Transdisciplinary Imperative** — 65
Adam Short
Soccer Coach, Richmond, Virginia

Chapter 6 **Beyond Western Eyes: Theorizing Feminism in the Indian Context** — 81
Chandrakala Padia
Professor, Department of Political Science, Banaras Hindu University, Varanasi

Chapter 7 **The Reconstruction of the Myth of Hindutva and the Great Indian Patriarchy** — 97
Guni Vats
Research Scholar, Department of English, University of Lucknow

Contributors — 117

Index — 119

Preface

The idea behind the present anthology *History and Myth: Postcolonial Dimensions* is to bring to the fore the postcolonial perspectives on myth and history with the help of select articles by scholars and researchers from across the globe. This book seeks to discover the truth and restore the national pride of the colonially subjugated nations by reclaiming the meaning of their past strengthened by their myths and histories. It is a known fact that our current understanding of histories and myths of the former European colonies is primarily influenced by the colonially fashioned binaries like civilized/barbaric, valid/invalid, inclusive/exclusive, relevant/irrelevant, true/false, good/bad, and many more. These binaries continue to preserve the epistemological and the ontological citadels of coloniality and selectively promote such narratives that celebrate the superiority of colonial/Western ideologies and the inferiority of Rest-ern beliefs and practices. In this view, the authors herein interrogate the templates of colonial/western histories and myths in a multidimensional manner.

A look into the history of colonialism informs us that the European expansion over India, China, Southeast Asia, the Americas, and Africa initially began as a commercial expedition but soon acquired the traits of cultural imperialism. The Industrial Revolution resulted in an economic acceleration in Europe, which increased the demand for colonial expansion and naval control. In due course of time, it transformed the entire world into a ready market for the British manufacturers, which increased the need for technologies, discoveries, advanced modes of transport, new laws, and regulations to fulfill the trade needs.

The growing wealth of Europe was inversely proportional to the economic condition of Asia, Africa, and other colonies as they lost their power and glory under colonial impact and consequently became geographically, politically, and culturally subjugated. Hence, Europe continued to emerge as a reliable economic and military power that infused a sense of superiority in its people. The colonizers began to feel insurmountable and had a natural right to rule over the non-Europeans. This situation resulted in the racial supremacy of the Whites and developed in them the illusion that it was their responsibility being white men to civilize the inferior people of color residing in the non-European countries. Thus, the industrial mission, by and large, became civilizational, and the coercive and illegitimate measures began to be employed by the masters to teach and civilize the non-Europeans. This civilizational burden divided the world into three categories – civilized, uncivilized, and barbaric, in which the Europeans represented the first category.

The principles of Christian morality became a prominent tool in the execution of civilizational missions and the strengthening of the imperial forces. The European colonizers exercised the agenda of church and colonization through various doctrinal means, such as the Papal Bull, *Terra Nullius*, Capitulation, the discovery of new lands, assault on indigeneity, and misuse of the rule of law. Papal Bull was a kind of public decree or charter issued by the Pope of the Catholic Church to encourage the kings to conquer the undiscovered lands, enslave their non-Christian populations and acquire their resources. The doctrine of discovery strengthened the project of colonization which sanctified genocide besides attacking the land and indigeneity of those people. Likewise, the colonizers unlawfully obtained many territories through the exercise of the doctrine of *Terra Nullius*. By considering the lands owned by non-Christians as *Terra Nullius* (nobody's land), this principle gave the Christian kingdoms of Europe a legitimate grant to claim and kill non-Europeans and non-Christians. The capitulation was another measure to annex territories through a unilateral pact, contract, or treaty by which a sovereign state gives away jurisdiction within its borders over the subjects of a foreign state. The Europeans' tools and strategic measures to conquer over others proved more effective than launching any battle. Above all, a decisive nail in the coffin was the historical Vienna Congress of 1815. With this, Europe declared itself the international legislator and hijacked laws to exercise aggressive imperialism.

The Christian missionaries that went to Africa promised the natives to show them the path of salvation by gifting a copy of the Bible. They acquired their land and territory, and declared Africa a dark continent by the 19th century. Similarly, Asia was portrayed as exotic, infidel, and vicious, and European colonizers developed various mechanisms to utilize this depiction to prove Asian culture inferior. This condition resulted in the mass killing and erasure of non-Christian natives and indigenous communities; their history, myths, rituals, traditions, language, and religion, along with their geopolitical identities. Knowing this helps us understand how the various forms of indigenous histories and myths have been dehumanized, and how the colonial/Western constructed narratives have undergone universal propagations across different segments of time and space.

It is pretty evident that the colonial masters not only imposed their language, culture, tradition, religion, lifestyle, and food habits on the subjugated people during colonialism and imperialism, but they also gave their interpretation of the history, culture, and myth of the indigenous people in the name of civilizing them. With a *modus operandi* to rule over others, they boasted of their racial superiority and induced inferiority in the minds of the colonized people.

Consequently, the subjugated people were forced to forget their national pride and accept the terms and conditions of slavery and capitulation imposed on them. In the post-second world war period, the independence of Afro-Asian countries brought about a kind of national awakening in the newly independent nation-states. At the same time, the postcolonial movement in humanities and social sciences in the form of discourses also gained a slow but steady momentum. One welcome outcome of this was the revival of the interest of the third world scholars in having a fresh look at their history, myth, culture, knowledge, and practices to redefine, restructure, and resurrect the same in a pristine manner to the extent possible.

Postcolonial consciousness, which emerged as a reaction to Eurocentrism, sought to produce counter-narratives to the grand narratives structured, imposed, and inserted in the non-European nations by the colonial masters. It has been realized over the years that the deeply rooted colonialism cannot be dislodged so easily unless and until the native history, myth, and culture of the former colonies are revived, regained, and re-established. Decolonial thinking and doing in this regard may be seen as a systematic study to analyze the theory, praxis, and politics of colonization. The voices of non-Western countries favor the redefinition of their identity and the need for self-determination to be articulated with great force. Hence, in recent years, postcolonial and decolonial discourses have gained much currency, and scholars and researchers in this field have given their best to dissolve the binaries erected by the West.

The book contains seven chapters based on the intensive and extensive study on the issues related to myth and history from postcolonial perspectives. It has been broadly divided into two sections. Section one, titled "Postcolonialism and/in Texts: Histories and Myths," contains four essays reflecting on the issues related to material development and human regression, postcolonial imaginary, ancient stories, and their current praxes; whereas the second section, "Decoloniality: Experiences and Engagements" discusses in detail the issues related to race, reconstruction of the myth of Hindutva, the notion of Indian patriarchy, dehierarchization and decolonization of postcolonial existence, and the Indian way of feminism from postcolonial perspectives. A separate and independent chapter as an introduction to this book has been written by Waseem Anwar, who offers critical exposition and theoretical account of the theme of the present work. It is followed by the essays of different authors who provide a new understanding of the history, myth, culture, tradition, etc.

Diptarup Ghosh Dastidar's chapter "Material Development and Human Regression: A Decolonial Reading of Orijit Sen's *River of Stories*" reflects how capital and capital-generating resources widely contributed to the evolution of

European colonialism in India. To justify the arguments, the author analyzes the conflicting lifestyles depicted in Orijit Sen's graphic novel *River of Stories* (1994). The novel's narrative deals with the construction of the Rewa Sagar dam and the reactions against it by the locals, as seen by a journalist from *Voice* who goes to cover the story. A parallel narrative voice of Malgu Gayan, the village singer, adds a fantastical element to the report by creating a myth-oriented history of the setting, which is then challenged by colonial voices, where history and facts have tampered to justify actions against the natives.

"A Tale of Things: Decoloniality of Memory in Orhan Pamuk's *The Museum of Innocence*" by Chand Basha explores the geopolitical memory of the city and its cultural location in the era of globalization in Pamuk's novel published in 2009. The article precisely addresses the lived experiences on the edge of Europe, the orientalist perspective attributed to it, and the decolonial gestures of Pamuk. While addressing the question of decolonizing the museum, the author clarifies that the process of decolonizing the museum does not propose the idea of eliminating museum culture from the axiomatic trajectory of the aesthetic and critical representation of cultures. However, it seeks to transform the museum as a source of story and space narratives. Altogether, Pamuk's criticism of the flashy stories of native cultures has been analytically highlighted, which opens another space between the decolonial museum and personal museum.

The chapter "Post-9/11, Cultural Amnesia and Representation(s) of Islamophobia in Ayad Akhtar's *Disgraced*" by Abhisek Ghosal highlights the playwright's emphasis on the interactions among postcolonial ambivalence, security, and transnational resistance to divulge the possibility of putting up the global resistance to the act of distortion as practiced by the United States. Further, the essay interrogates as well as deflates the efforts of Akhtar to build up a postcolonial imaginary. The study shows that the play is a rant on Islamophobic discourses that are sponsored and propagated, according to the playwright, by the US authorities on the Muslim immigrants. The author also argues that Akhtar has taken up representational politics at a crucial moment when the US launches a war on terror policy and puts cultural amnesia at work.

Feroza Jussawalla's chapter "Ancient Stories, Current Praxes: Decolonial Myths in Contemporary Literature" posits that myths have always had a decolonial purpose of connecting culture with its indigenous or local stories both at the moment of contact and in the moments of stress. The scholar has attempted to distinguish between the notions of decolonial and decolonizing by underlining that the decolonial moment is the moment of interaction and awareness that later on leads to decolonizing. The author also refers to the Mexican myth of La Llorona through *The Little Mermaid* and instances from

Joyce to D.H. Lawrence (who also uses Mexican myths) to underscore the importance of the female voice in the liberation of the other.

The chapter "White as Paper, Black as Ink: Bilali Muhammad and the Transdisciplinary Imperative" by Adam Short studies the epic tale of Bilali Muhammad and identifies the tropes this story violates. It reveals how such stories are being prevented from being told even when Hollywood is looking for scripts that incorporate themes of black liberation. Further, it shows how the distinct Muslim characters of the Bilali Muhammad story make it incredibly dissonant with the fictionalized version of black history, usually presented by Hollywood. The author believes that it is necessary to transcend the boundaries of various academic disciplines and participate in preserving and perpetuating cultures.

The chapter "Beyond Western Eyes: Theorizing Feminism in the Indian Context" by Chandrakala Padia attempts to construct an Indian theory of feminism and foregrounds how due to ethnocentric and Eurocentric biases present in the Western Feminist discourse, an Indian theory of feminism could not evolve the way it should have; however, there was no shortage of literary and sociological writings in both classical and modern languages of India. The argument uncovers the misreading of ancient Indian texts by many Western as well as Indian scholars. It also brings to the fore how these scholars have distorted the meaning of *parampara* (tradition) in the Indian worldview, which led to the false representations of Indian and Third World Women, and how their limited understanding of the Sanskrit language led to wrong translations of Indian texts leading to the justification of many unhealthy practices in the Indian society.

The final chapter of this edited volume is Guni Vats' "The Reconstruction of the Myth of Hindutva and the Great Indian Patriarchy." It endeavors to read contemporary India's political scenario as a text to study how myths have been exploited to construct new Indian patriarchy. Every intellectual is busy saving the constitution, and women are on the back foot. Here, the postcolonial issues have been analyzed from the patriarchal perspective. The author believes that the semiology of myth dictates a specific meaning that is more often colored with hierarchy bias. The symbols are already loaded with hierarchical explanations, and the process of deciphering their intentions also clung to the structure responsible for constructing them.

The anthology, on the whole, is a humble attempt to enrich our understanding of postcolonial consciousness because of myth and history concerning theory, practice, and politics. The topics covered in this volume have regional and global relevance as they unravel the complex layers of biasedly framed narratives. Therefore, the anthology offers a symphony of select chapters expressive of diverse opinions from different spatiotemporal zones at one place. Since it is difficult to cover all the dimensions of the postcolonial studies in a single book, only special issues have been taken up by the authors to indicate the possibility of new researches. We hope that this volume would make a meaningful contribution to the enrichment of existing studies and research in this area.

In accomplishing this book project, the contribution and support of many people need to be sincerely acknowledged. Professor B.C. Nirmal, Law School, Banaras Hindu University and former Vice-Chancellor, National University of Study and Research in Law, Ranchi (India) and Professor Chandrakala Padia, Department of Political Science, Banaras Hindu University, former Vice-Chancellor, Maharaja Ganga Singh University, Bikaner, and former Chairman, Governing Body, Indian Institute of Advanced Study, Shimla (India) suggested the idea of editing a volume of this kind. We are thankful to them for their encouragement and support. We feel indebted to Professor Diana Fox, Chairperson of Anthropology, Bridgewater State University, Massachusetts, for gracing the book with her illuminating Foreword and Professor Waseem Anwar, Forman Christian College Lahore, Pakistan, for contributing a highly comprehensive introduction to this volume. We feel incredibly grateful to Shankhadeep Chattopadhyay and Kathakali Sengupta for patiently and thoroughly proofreading the manuscript. We also express our gratitude to the authors interested in the present study who contributed their articles to be anthologized herein. The Vernon Press, USA, and its entire editorial team extended all possible support in the publication of this book. Their contribution is humbly acknowledged.

July 2021

Arti Nirmal

Sayan Dey

Foreword

Diana J. Fox

Bridgewater State University,
Massachusetts

The present collection pertains to myth and history. It includes an eclectic array of creative chapters adopting both postcolonial and decolonial frames to analyze a play, a novel, an ambiguously ethnic neighborhood, a novel about a museum, mythological narratives vis-à-vis the patriarchal state, a legal document crafted by a Muslim slave in North America, a critically reflective comic strip, the nature of lived-experience and more. The book is organized into two segments, first "Postcolonialism and/in Texts: Histories and Myths," followed by "Decoloniality: Experiences and Engagements." Together, these themes indicate the editors' intention of demonstrating the far reach of decoloniality into multiple arenas of cultural life and production.

The editors' pressing political purview is also clear: decoloniality is a necessary and urgent praxis for revealing and condemning the long reach of colonial distortions that have caused great suffering. Decolonial praxis is a prerequisite to building equitable and sustainable societies. Diptarup Ghosh Dastidar, in his chapter on "Material Development and Human Regression: A Decolonial Reading of Orjit Sen's *River of Stories*," a story in comic-book format, observes that the comic book serves as a form of visuality that humanizes the wretched and communicates sensitive concerns like human dignity and value for life. There is an idea gaining ground across the social and life sciences promoted by Julia Rhoher, a personality psychologist at the Max Planck Institute for Human Development, called "intellectual humility, the characteristic that allows for the admission of wrongness" (cited in Resnick 5). In a 2019 article about intellectual humility, Brian Resnick explains: "People who score higher on intellectual humility questionnaires are more open to hearing opposing views. They more readily seek out information that conflicts with their worldview. They pay more attention to evidence and have a stronger self-awareness when they answer a question incorrectly" (4). I find an exciting and essential overlap between the purviews of post- and decolonial scholars and intellectual humility: it is a necessary ingredient to challenge the matrix of ideologies that have created a vast hierarchical world of enormous inequality. Those who wish to preserve this inequality the most have the least intellectual humility—which tells us something about the kind of mindset training that decolonial pedagogies must adopt. Over time, these accounts have built portraits of those who came "under western eyes" (Mohanty 334) that not only ignore and undermine pre-colonial worlds but twist and deform peoples' conceptions of themselves through what Gayatri Spivak has referred to as epistemic violence.

How is this collection relevant to what is happening right now in the world, as I write at my kitchen table in Providence, Rhode Island, a space that has been the epicenter of so many women's political activist movements? The world is in the global Covid-19 pandemic, a viral pathogen in company with other pandemics—SARS, Ebola, of the relatively recent past, with more to come, as climate crisis melts the arctic permafrost into our planet's shrinking biodiversity. Growing inequalities wrack the world, billionaires profiteering off the virus, but at the same time, the world's struggling majority is not sitting passively. Instead, we are in the midst of what many are calling the second civil rights movement in my own country. Black Lives Matter protests reverberate across the country, and mediascapes stimulate solidarity with like-minded protests, highlighting regional concerns such as Dalit Lives Matter marches in India and Nepal. In Portland, Oregon, a cross-section of the population spills into the streets to confront federal agents, Department of Homeland Security forces, deployed by the Trump administration to quash the protests. Fascism, nativism, and authoritarianism are rising globally from Brazil to India, across Europe, and back to the United States. And how are US universities responding? Many, including my own, are finally mobilizing into systemic action to bring about decolonized curricula and institutions, supporting platforms and widely distributed anti-racist and decolonial syllabi launched by this collective Black, Indigenous, and People of Color (BIPOC) social movement. This collection of chapters is suited ideally to be incorporated into these new decolonial syllabi across multiple disciplines.

The chapters reintroduce readers to many of the renowned writers in the field, including Frantz Fanon, Edward Said, Homi Bhabha, Gayatri Spivak, Anibal Quijano, and others, while bringing together many other scholarly voices specific to the particular topics of their chapters. This bibliographical expansion—including the authors of the chapters themselves—is one of the gifts of this volume not only to those specializing in the decolonial project as a genre of analysis but in the broader challenge that decoloniality poses to us in our historical moment: to remake a livable, sustainable world by continuing to conceptualize and actualize decolonial methodology.

Many of the chapters scrutinize 19th and 20th-century British colonial practices and ideologies. Yet, there is the clear implication that these are themselves products of a more extended foundational imperial history that demands unpacking. This is no easy undertaking since one of the most pernicious outcomes of colonialism is the hegemony of positivist, objectivist, heteronormative thought that has undermined, obfuscated, and delegitimized pre-colonial, Indigenous ways of knowing and knowledge categories. At the same time, colonial knowledge systems were systematically entangled with particular, decontextualized features of pre-colonial thought and practice, reifying them as fixed in the historical and contemporary landscapes. This reality renders the decolonial project inordinately complex. It is tasked with reconstructing pre-colonial worlds of thought and practice and placing them into the flow of history with their contemporary liberatory possibilities through cultural revitalization movements. Therefore, the process of understanding the colonial psyche is a critical step in the creation of social movements that do not reproduce colonial mindsets or narratives that produce colonial renditions of history.

By way of example, it helps think about the value of the decolonial lens to consider how it can be helpful to understand that before British colonialism, India was characterized by a pluralistic, fragmented, cultural, and religious political structure in which there was no monolithic Hindu, Muslim or Christian authority. With the support of British power, the Hindu law expanded its lead across large areas of society that had not known it before "the codification movement of the 1880s brought the castes and tribes that were traditionally outside the Varna system into the Hindu fold, thereby broadening the scope of the Hindu law at a time when there was no real uniform understanding of the term Hindu" (Abraham 68-69).

This cementing of Hindu law was critical to fomenting and normalizing Hindu nationalism, which both fosters a mainly Indian version of Islamophobia and is intertwined with patriarchy, as Guni Vats argues in his chapter, "The Reconstruction of the Myth of Hindutva and the Great Indian Patriarchy." Vats refer to Parashuram, a masculine Hindu epitome, a revered Vishnu incarnation [who] became a crucial mythical character in realizing a Hindu national male identity. Tracing the ideological origins of this revivalist-nationalist tradition remains crucial to understanding contemporary Indian politics, particularly regarding the status of women and the problem of recent Hindu-Muslim violence. Vats focuses specifically on the ideological role of mythology in creating a Hindu patriarchal identity. At the same time, Sarkar argues that material changes in Indian society that introduced insecurity to middle-class landholders, squeezing them out of markets through British colonial policies, were also critical elements in forming Hindu nationalist patriarchy.

This feminist critique is critical in demonstrating that reconstructing pre-colonial and colonial realities is a necessary step in understanding contemporary hierarchies and their associated ideologies. Still, more than this, those contested accounts are part of the process of reviving Indigenous ways of knowing and narrating the world. Linda Tuhiwai Smith explains in *Decolonizing Methodologies:*

Research and Indigenous Peoples (1999) that "the idea of contested stories and multiple discourses about the past, by different communities, is closely linked to the politics of everyday contemporary indigenous life. It is very much a part of the fabric of communities that value oral ways of knowing" (33). Similarly, the decolonial lens is an opening for contestation among decolonial scholars to debate with one another, which is what I have sought to mirror here in the above explication, demonstrating the potential of this collection of essays toward robust decolonial debates across disciplines. One fascinating example of this methodology in the group is Adam Short's chapter, "Inadmissible Blackness: Bilali Muhammad and the Transdisciplinary Imperative." Through careful attention to historiographical reconstruction, drawing on archives, diaries, literature, and films (particularly Toni Morrison's *Song of Solomon* and Julie Dash's *Daughters of the Dust*), Short unwinds more than two centuries of biased and false narratives surrounding the 19th-century Bilali Muhammad's *Meditations*.

Together, the chapters illuminate a range of epistemological strategies for constructing decolonial narratives. These included positioning the author's processes of inquiry and reflection as a challenge to the obfuscation of subjectivity in the educational process, a challenge that feminist thinkers have posed since the 1970s to assumptions of pure objectivity and introduced into decolonial methodologies. For example, feminist theorist Donna Haraway, in her essay, "Situated Knowledges: The Science Question in Feminism and the Privilege of Partial Perspective" (1988), has sought to eradicate what she calls the "god trick" (580) – the positivist assumption that the knowledge of white Euro/American masculinity is universal instead of being situated.

I hope this foreword has offered readers a tantalizing taste through a few examples of what is to come as readers make their way through the chapters, unpacking and dismantling the many intertwining branches of colonialism through post- and decolonial scholarly praxis. In so doing, I urge readers to take steps toward embracing intellectual humility, a process that opens us up to knowing beyond our beliefs. In closing, I would like to encourage readers to reflect on some of the achievements of decoloniality and where we have yet to go. The recognition of this and other deep wisdom surfaced through decoloniality that this book seeks to impress upon us.

2021

Diana J. Fox

Professor and Chair, Department of Anthropology
Bridgewater State University, Massachusetts

Works Cited

Abraham, Kochurani. *Persisting Patriarchy: Intersectionalities, Negotiations, Subversions.* Palgrave Macmillan, 2019. Print.

Haraway, Donna. "Situated Knowledges: The Science Question in Feminism and the Privilege of Partial Perspective." *Feminist Studies* 14.3 (1988): 575-99. Print.

Mohanty, Chandra Talpade. "Under Western Eyes: Feminist Scholarship and Colonial Discourses." *Boundary 2* 13.3 (1984): 333-58. Print.

Resnick, Brian. "Intellectual Humility: The Importance of Knowing You Might Be Wrong." *Vox*, 04 Apr. 2019, www.vox.com/science-and-health/2019/1/4/17989224/intellectual-humility-explained-psychology-replication.

Tuhiwai Smith, Linda. *Decolonizing Methodologies: Research and Indigenous Peoples.* Zed, 1999. Print.

Introduction - Decolonization and its Discontents: Democratization, Demarcations, Dangers

Waseem Anwar

Forman Christian College, Lahore

Perhaps ... postcoloniality ... is a fluid, polysemic, and ambiguous term ... seen situationally ... in terms of Gramscian conjuncturalism ... Yet ... postcolonial societies [are] ... political categories ... which conceal hegemonic assumptions ... [while] Decolonization ... is ... a struggle over categories.

(Coronil 200-204)

I believe, in the strident journalistic debates about decolonization, in which imperialism is repeatedly on record as saying, in effect, you are what you are because of us; when we left, you reverted to your deplorable state; know that or you will know nothing, for certainly there is little to be known about imperialism that might help either you or us in the present.

(Said 30)

Decolonization is what I call a theory of life. Embedded in decolonization are colonial wounds crying out for healing. Decolonization encapsulates possibilities of creating another world.

(Ndlovu-Gatsheni 32)

Knowing that there are innumerable dimensions related to the ongoing struggles of decolonization, yet given the title of this Introduction (or Reintroduction), one may inquire instantly: Why look for discontents, and for what purpose; aspiration, approximation, or appropriation? I have neither of the intents nor am I using discontent in terms of discomfort, dismay, remorse, or what Sigmund Freud would urge, a desire's instinctive conflict with conformity or unhappiness with the "social and civilizational repression" (Freud 5-6). I instead exploit discontent as a notion for possible conjunctive categorization that may examine the somewhat indeterminate expansion of decolonization. The anxious and at times apprehensive processes of decolonization invite many crossroads when it comes to exploring its conceptual complicity, the sociocultural, spatio-temporal, aesthetical, or literary engagement that qualifies it to be a continuing condition, a de-colonialism augmenting from what we popularly pronounce as the colonial and its associates; colonialism, colonialization, coloniality, colony, its synonyms, and antonyms, so on and so forth. While the colonial is assumptively an outcome of some cosmological or theological sensibility to overpower, dominate and control, decolonial does denote an opposite; a liberating if not democratizing resistance to domination for control. However, what are the parameters, precincts, tethers, traces, or trajectories of the imagined territoriality of decolonization; the domain, diameters and demarcations of its free spirit and the resultant dilemmas or dangers, stays so ambiguous that it is at such crossroads and crisscrosses that decolonization proliferates the open-ended-ness of its periodization.

Whether all the de-s, pre-s, or posts in literary, critical, and theoretical schmooze have their discontents related to examination, containment or expansion of periodization, be it deconstruction, decentralization, demythologization, postmodernism, poststructuralism, precolonialism, or postcolonialism, the imperviousness for anyone debating decolonization may relate to the presumption that decolonization is a hyphenated phenomenon, the hyphen observed or not, a 'de-' tagged to its connotative 'of,' 'to' or 'from' for suggesting reversal, recovery, retribution, retaliation or relegation though not necessarily and always regression. And then its entwined theoretical upsurge along the colonial and postcolonial experience, its etymological and historical meaningfulness interwoven with the lingering colonial after-effects allows a concurring position with or without hyphenation, consenting decolonization to be a unified whole, at once for all anti- and reprisal. So, does such a (dis)placement of the prefix 'de' or the hyphen next to it affect its meaning-making, if it does, or does it not matter at all?

But the prefix 'de' with colonization, hyphenated or not, intrinsically implies multiple other prefixes and suffixes attached to diverse historical transpiration within colonialism and its over-prolonged condition. Though the notion of decolonization occurs as an integral part of the postcolonial enunciation, within the context, colonialism does offer a contentious conjuncture for decolonization and its possible democratization, a spot not only for its freedom but also its disagreement, displacement, dispersal, dissent, discontent, and danger. This contact zone results from more divisiveness than unionization.

And therefore, decolonization, before it shapes into any conceptual framework, invites dialogic intervention of the colonial, while its 'de-'ing processes initiate fluctuating entanglement with its fixities, fixtures, and fixations to map its various scopes; called they might be ambivalent, amorphous, ill-defined, well-defined or else wise. The de, pre-, post-, neo-, re-, -ization, -ized, -ity, etc. etc., as they are diametrically employed around, before or after the colonial under diverse ensuing circumstances, open avenues for deliberations arriving nowhere, somewhere, anywhere or everywhere. Whatever complexities the 'de' of the colonial engage in its historicization and theorization, it concedes decolonization to move back and forth in time and space though apparently and always forward into a future.

That the three-fourth of the globe was once physically colonized is a geographical, historical, and political fact. This axiomatic truth no more needs evidential explications, while there have been pre-colonial civilizational histories of conquest as well, equally smothered with battle and brutality. In contrast, Postcolonial Studies and its discursive mode employs openly and in specific the stories about Post-Renaissance European colonial expansion, its plunder, loot, and racist and sexist ideological abuses above 400 years, because it counts on a comparatively more settled periodization of the human history of imperial and economic coercion, the overseeing system imposed by foreigners and settlers upon natives, by aliens on land belonging to the locals or aboriginals. Whether the connectivity between colonial and postcolonial has been taught from the right or wrong sides, the catapult of the pre- to postcolonial conversations remains an enticing sphere for possible conflictual negotiation and meaning-making, leading to extensive debates decolonization and its fretfully evolving strategies and techniques. As a project, decolonization has been described by various experts as an enduring pursuit into relearning, rethinking, re-theorizing, redefining, and rediscovering what might have been ignored, neglected, concealed, or misconceived, or even wrongfully communicated and propagated. And this is also in terms of reassigning the positions of power and negotiation and their relation to the centralized or decentralized loci, be it for debating the knowledge sources or interrogating the essential human-subhuman existential hierarchies.

Under the Postcolonial Studies, decolonization, as we find it interpreted initially per *Britannica*, remains a 20th-century mobilizing movement that attempts to reverse the colonial powers and their discriminatory territorialization. If, on the one hand, it is an attempt to read and research colonialism as the external as well as internal "intimate enemy" (41), to use Ashis Nandy's oxymoronic coinage, it also goes to the extent where it keeps scrutinizing what Samir Amin phrases, the extraversion of its sociopolitical economies. Whether decolonization could or could not de-territorialize the colonial geo-histories for recovering the origin proves a cartographic and cultural failure that may be tagged to various political, economic, linguistic, technological, or cultural losses other factors. For a theorist like Frantz Fanon, decolonization evolves to be prehistoric, a prenatal phenomenon that encounters "between two congenitally antagonistic forces" (31), resulting in later aggressions and actions. Decolonization for Fanon then remains a "ferocious and violent activity" (13). Not going that far, decolonization, as Bill Ashcroft, Gareth Griffiths, and Helen Tiffin describe, attempts to dismantle the post-independence remnants along with their "hidden aspects of ... [the colonialist's] institutional and cultural forces" (56-59), resulting in a mimic, hybrid or hegemonic existence that continues struggles to promote indigeneity and nativism even against the latest postcolonial imperial designs like neocolonialism or globalization.

Decolonization then, above all, even if not leading to collective nationalistic independence or individual freedom, emerges in various new global, regional or local patterns as some reflection upon the frames of what John McLeod pronounces, an imagined "colonial demise" (6). However, even if this demise could happen or not, with its inferences related to resettling the settlements, equalizing the economic and other inequalities, or re-managing the governance power-games, colonialism did lose its corporeal and slavish foothold because of the postcolonial activism and consciousness among the people who were once physically occupied. But, its repercussions prevailing in proportions, colonialism, and its imperialistic designs stemmed in setting the ground for postcolonial embarkation of the decolonization projects, letting them happen in historical successions for indigenous and native empowerment. The expectation then, of course, relates to dispelling the ideological systematization or diversification of the postcolonial philosophies and practices that continue to pick on issues across the globe, including provincializing, de-provincializing, or re-provincializing of the continents, reframing the other from multiple neutralist perspectives, reassessing the postcolonial nationalisms from multi-nationalistic standpoints, re-evaluating the nominal and pronominal perceptions of them and us.

Though such infringing and intersectional contravention to democratize the decolonizing nations and notions through post-independence movements against oppression tempts one to jump into the polemics extended by Edward Said's *Orientalism*, Ashcroft's *The Empire Writes Back*, Gauri Viswanathan's *Masks of Conquest*, Homi K. Bhabha's notions of the nation and its narration, and Robert J. C. Young's appropriations of the colonial mythology and its conflating structures, yet we try not to get lured by so many similar tantalizing predicaments. Our goal here is not to track the combated colonial discourses but to re-search their sublimations through conflictual-attitudinal representational modes that regain a de-territorialized and democratized consciousness from the many forms of postcolonial experiences. What we are trying to focus on is to read the implication that our passing from colonial to postcolonial and decolonial scape has been through the phases related to transference of power among hierarchies of populations, be they indigenous, internalized, or [in]visible in terms of race, gender, sexuality, religion, creed, caste or numerous other categories of inequity. In this context, one may sense that the binary between the colonial and its post- has not truly been indemnified by the multiple processes imbued within the prefix post-, de- or their prefixation with the colonization as well as decolonization of the peripheral, also reminding us that we still need to explore multiple other sides of the colonial currency that has camouflaged control and cruelty behind hegemonic systems of giving and take or divide and rule. So along with many complicated conditions, the experience of post-independence decolonization, its dynamics of the associated democratization brings us to a point where we cannot resist reechoing Fanon's retrieval for defying the antagonistic attitudes or Ngugi wa Thiong'o's finding of decolonizing not just the body but "the mind" (71). Based on their theoretical stances for political cum cultural resistance, Fanon's and Ngugi's suggestions to deconstruct, decenter, and decolonize the centric intellectual sovereignties and their base may be argued as an ultimate goal. Still, we also need and dare to ask upfront: whose interest decolonization might be serving and what?

To dare to question decolonization and its procedures and practices is to raise our postcolonial consciousness and understand the validity of discontents and dangers that the post-independence codes of democratization among decolonizing countries may signify. While the scholarly calls of the decolonization experts, like Simon Gikandi's demand for questioning the very foundations and tools of national narratives, Dennis Walder's urge to revisit the representations of postcolonial nostalgias and memories, Nelson Maldonado-Torres' rethinking and re-theorization through the decolonial turn, Walter Mignolo's exploration of the geopolitics of knowledge, cultural decolonization, Eurocentric renaissance and alternative literacies, Ramon Grosfoguel's study of racial decolonization, migrations, Islamophobia and world political-economies, Boaventuro de Sousa Santos' decolonization of epistemologies and knowledge hubs to challenge the deeper cognitive empires or Ndlovu-Gatsheni's inquiry into colonial encounters, democracies and the myths of decolonization suggest us to re-interrogate the prefix post- in postcolonial. What has then democracy and the codes of democratization, its demarcations, and diameters to do with the processes of decolonization, and why do we need to talk about them? Is our [post]independence freedom meant for all those unfettered in the name of decolonization? Such questions relate to the persistently colonized jeopardy of the minorities; classes, genders, ethnicities, religions or sects, etc.; women, gays, lesbians, daily-wagers, believers, atheists, or many others. Suppose for the scholars of colonialism, the physical of the colonial recedes to foreground its metaphysical significance. In that case, the scholars of decolonization must cross-examine the phenomenon of decolonization to trace its ongoing confiscatory, discriminatory, restrictive, or reductive practices that continue to obscure its democratizing processes? Our dream appended to post-independence democracies through decolonization is the dream of freedom with dignity. For such ideals of equality, justice, tolerance, and peace, all the decolonizing democratic institutions must work. Decolonization is about the basic human autonomies, communal civilities, and individual contentment.

While the focus of *History and Myth: Postcolonial Dimensions* is on the indigenous and internal politics, especially the much-internalized politics of decolonization, its theory, praxis, and myth-making, the hinge of the colonial upon its [de]hyphenated 'post' and 'de' in terms of purporting an after, extension or anti, serves as a powerful backdrop for debates, deliberations, and discussions in this volume. The chapters here reflect an effort to roll back the myths about colonial histories and stories, but they are also an accounted means to raise readers' autonomy and awareness. From binary to beyond, West-centric to East-oriented, white, black or brown, or the self-other dynamics, these essays explore our post-colonially constructed stories, while ingrained with the multi-theoretical conceptualization of decolonization and playing around the politics of postcolonial praxis contentions, the scholars writing for the volume realize a need for more transcultural vision about human heritage and its globally impacting psyches. In a way, the writings mirror our Self through the other or vice versa. Reviewing the in-fashion postcolonial consciousness and flouting the hierarchies of borrowed, mimicked, or hybridized attitudes, these writings vow a revival of the indigenous narratives so that the general discursive practice of the decolonized voices offers an existential platform of freedom for all to agree or disagree.

As the multi-positional themes and topics challenge our postcolonial imaginaries by raising concern about centered colonial influences that still overwhelm the global consciousness, we are led to contextualize the various forms of economic and cultural inferiority. Some of the chapters challenge post-9/11 identities, ambivalence, surveillance, and security that distort cultural traits. There are issues raised about racial and ethnic liberation to counter the strategic erasure of communities from big screens under the biases of colonial and decolonial cultural co-constructs. Comparison is also drawn on how traditional symbols of communication and their agency operate in African films or how the South African decolonizing projects approach colonial histories skeptically to foreground the African feminist decolonial praxes. As we look critically at the artificiality of prevailing Western cultures, we explore

Eastern cultures conserved in the museums. There are arguments about how conflicting lifestyles are presented through graphic novels, how the Fascist preoccupations or Western feminist notions are challenged in the more ancient mythologies and their profound decolonial moments, and how Antigone's heterotopia is redefined in a tele-ontological crisis. Research in the volume also delves into post-partition secularism in South Asian plays that counter the overwhelming religious ideologies and new power connections between ideologies like Hindutva and patriarchy. Studies are also done on contemporary post-truth politics that plays around media, myth, and memory to comment on feminist performance texts, emphasizing revisiting the traditions that reinforce rather than rarefy the Eurocentric colonial consciousness. Resultantly, examining ontological rights and possibilities for dissolving hierarchies to generate pluri-versal frameworks are an essential component of the volume.

With such a wide range of post-colonially and transcultural conscious placement, the book *History and Myth* invites its readers to idealize a decolonized democratic domain that endows citizenry privileges, personal freedoms, equal economic opportunity, social justice, intellectual autonomy, and various other forms of *laissez-faire* for the protection of demos and denizens. It asks us to observe and challenge our own colonizing and controlling tendencies, the divide within us, even when we all claim to be decolonizing the colonized. Though not with any heightened sense of guilt but its consciousness, and not precisely mastering our disturbances through what Freud would forewarn as instinctual awareness about being on the right and wrong sides of the postcolonial civilization, our looking for the discontents and dangers come along the post- and de- of colonial experiences to oscillate ourselves between then and now, helping us to move forward for a prospective neutral space. The chapters in this volume thus survey sociocultural validity of myths and realities about the colonial and its re-positioning if not [re]appropriation. They do let us question the directions, distinctions, and numerous diametrical posts of the center from many marginalized sites, allowing an investigation of the margin itself. That the processes of culturally more inclusive decolonization need to be tagged to the decolonial democratization becomes a prerequisite if the readers expect to dispel discontents and dangers. Specifically, this book lets us determine the shaped, de-shaped and re-shaped diameters of decolonization and exposes its more profound multidimensional universality. It foregrounds the entanglement of 'de' with double, triple, or manifold colonization so that its spatio-temporal vertical or horizontal movements remind us that the ghost of the colonialism was once there, and now its shadows, yet the spirit and its shadow need to be pushed further into oblivion. Suppose this comes to us as a Freudian sense of guilt about teaching the history and myth of decolonization from unifocal fringes. In that case, some deconstruction through such discontents may stay constructive and productive.

But, as pronounced at the outset of this Introduction, the demarcation of the readers' engagement with decolonization through projects like *History and Myth* offers a self-reflective caveat: How far to go and for what purpose? Does decolonial dismantling mean demolishing all the historical signs and symbols that we now [need to] own to be ours – the institutions, architectures, modified political and administrative systems, languages or cultures; also the English Departments that Ngugi wa Thiong'o had wanted us way back to abolish? Split amid the doldrums of owning-disowning, the question as to how decolonization of the cultural artifacts is possible remains debatable? For example, how to decolonize the practical value of English as a global *lingua franca* that Ismail S. Talib would describe as the source of "national unity ... [and] ... national development" (109), and that we also use as our means to share decolonized thought processes; how to neutralize the importance of English amid its continentally acknowledged diversity? Are we also asking for the abolishment of all our foreign languages (English) Departments? Somewhat offensive, but does being decolonial in such regressive ways imply going back to our invasive adulterations or fundamentalist dispossessions – at times our cannibalistic capitalisms in the form of caste systems, *sati* traditions, or the slavishly bonded labors? What is the filtration process that is required for us to decolonize what is to be decolonized truly? So picking on Fernando Coronil's description of situational postcolonialities, their fluidity, and polysemic ambiguity that many critics of Modernism, Postmodernism, and Postcolonialism refer to while relying on what Antonio Gramsci sees fringing in terms of "conjuncturalism" (cited in Coronil 201), the inclusive and strident debates in *History and Myth* seem to raise our understanding of decolonization amid the growing global, regional and communal inter-, intra-, cross as well as transcultural intersectionality for creating another world. Though the readings in *History and Myth* might still stay skeptical, they should be celebrated as another promising world for all those who partake in such enduring processes of decolonization.

Works Cited

Ashcroft, Bill, Gareth Griffiths, and Helen Tiffin. *Postcolonial Studies: The Key Concepts*. Routledge, 2007. Print.

Coronil, Fernando. "Can Postcoloniality Be Decolonized?" *Postcolonialism: Critical Concepts in Literary and Cultural Studies*. Ed. Diana Brydon. Routledge, 2000. 190-206. Print.

Fanon, Frantz. *The Wretched of the Earth*. Grove Press, 1961. Print.

Freud, Sigmund. *Civilization and its Discontents*. J. W. W. Norton & Co. Inc., 1961. Print.

McLeod, John. *Beginning Postcolonialism.* Manchester University Press, 2000. Print.

Nandy, Ashis. *The Intimate Enemy: Loss and Recovery of Self under Colonialism.* Oxford University Press, 1983. Print.

Ndlovu-Gatsheni, Sabelo J. "The Dynamics of Epistemological Decolonization in 21st Century: Towards Epistemic Freedom." *Strategic Review for Southern Africa* 40.1 (2018): 16-45.

Said, Edward. "Discrepant Experiences." *Postcolonial Discourses: An Anthology.* Ed. Gregory Castle. Wiley-Blackwell, 2001. 26-37. Print.

Talib, Ismail S. *The Language of Postcolonial Literatures: An Introduction.* Routledge, 2000. Print.

Thiong'o, Ngugi wa. *Decolonizing the Mind: The Politics of Language in African Literature.* James Currey, 1986. Print.

Part I
Postcolonialism and/ in Texts: Histories and Myths

Chapter 1

Material Development and Human Regression: A Decolonial Reading of Orijit Sen's *River of Stories*

Diptarup Ghosh Dastidar
Amity University, Raipur

Abstract

Colonial influence can be felt in the Indian consciousness as an idealistic fascination with Eurocentric notions of utility, work and leisure, broadly and wrongfully categorizing them as 'western' ideology. What affirms this belief in a 'western' order of existence is a feeling of economic and cultural inferiority. This feeling of inferiority is solidified by the visible differences in the choice of lifestyle – simplistic tribal life adhering to traditions that lack the intentional production of capital, or technocratic complex urban life surrounded by amenities and perks, which are available as rewards against 'work' done. In this chapter, I intend to present the above argument and show these conflicting lifestyles by analyzing the graphic novel *River of Stories* (1994) by Orijit Sen. The narrative is about the construction of Rewa Sagar dams and the reactions against it by the locals as seen by a journalist from *Voice* who goes to cover the story. A parallel narrative voice of Malgu Gayan, the village singer, adds a mythic element to the narrative. On that note, I discuss how the graphic novel takes a decolonial stand, pointing out certain futile elements of the Eurocentric notion of 'development.'

Keywords: colonial, decolonial, capital, graphic novel, ideology, myth, history.

* * *

"Memory believes before knowing remembers. Believes longer than recollects, longer than knowing even wonders."

(Faulkner 64)

Such is the power of belief that even though Faulkner, in the statement mentioned above, simply develops the setting for a flashback sequence, in reality, it speaks volumes about how the notion of coloniality works and how it is not just limited to a specific time-frame but applicable to human nature itself. Colonial relations depend vitally on the role played by memory in framing belief systems and hence, in hegemonizing the minds and actions/bodies of people belonging not only to a specific period but across numberless ensuing generations. This chapter engages in an understanding of the said colonial tensions through visual representations in comics within the context of Indian urban-tribal conflicts and is divided into two distinct sections. The first section briefly traces the scholarship around coloniality, differentiating it from colonialism and situating it as the con of modernity (which itself is defined in entirely Eurocentric terms), consequently understanding how decoloniality operates as an emancipatory tool for the victims ensnared by coloniality. The second section introduces Orijit Sen's *River of Stories* (here onwards as *RoS* for convenience) as a site where coloniality is practiced. It deliberates on how the graphic novel itself, both formalistically and structurally, takes a decolonial stand through quadruple pillars of myth, memory, voice, and topography — where decoloniality, as will be discussed below, is to be understood as a continual struggle and a constant state of resistance to agents of coloniality/modernity. These agents include, among others, all capitalist structures of thought, institutions, and episteme. While taking the stand, the chapter establishes how purely material terms are directly proportional to regression in the human element of what is understood as capitalist transactions.

From Colonialism to Coloniality

From the point of view of factors like temporality and *con*-sequentiality,[1] the differences between coloniality, colonialism, postcolonialism, and colonization need no further elucidation, given the extensive modernity/rationality/coloniality debate among decolonial scholars like Walter D. Mignolo ("de-linking") (451), Anibal Quijano ("coloniality of power") (540), Nelson Maldonado-Torres ("coloniality of being") (248), and Enrique Dussel ("trans-modernity and liberation") (35) among others. The arguments of these scholars take root in the ego-centered rationality of renaissance and enlightenment thinkers like Descartes and Kant, trudging through Heidegger ("*dasein*") (27) and Levinas ("face-to-face and the other") (89) to wind up in the territory of Fanon ("*damnés*") (245), and wa Thiong'o ("dismemberment") (5) holding the hands of Horkheimer ("critical theory") (9). To put otherwise, this tracing of epistemic traditions suggests how a division is made historically between two or more intelligent beings/races/communities based on power, which is sanctioned by capital, and how exploitation is possible with the lure of liberation and modernity. While colonialism is an established historical and time-specific phenomenon born out of European colonization and its subsequent colonial practices,

Maldonado-Torres defines it as "a political and economic relation in which the sovereignty of a nation or a people rests on the power of another nation, which makes such nation an empire" (243). Coloniality, on the other hand, "refers to long-standing patterns of power that emerged as a result of colonialism, but that define culture, labor, intersubjective relations, and knowledge production well beyond the strict limits of colonial administrations. Thus, coloniality survives colonialism" (Maldonado-Torres 243) and transcends the restraints of time and place, being born and thriving in zones of conflict.

Coloniality, Modernity, and Decoloniality

Evaluating the relationship between modernity and coloniality, Mignolo traces the roots of modernity to the introduction of new drugs like tobacco, caffeine, and glucose to replace alcohol in the European upper classes by referring to the works of Anthony Giddens on modernity and empire, respectively. To quote Giddens, "Modernity refers to modes of social life or organization which emerged in Europe from about the seventeenth century onwards and which subsequently became more or less worldwide in their influence. This associates modernity with a period and with an initial geographical location" (1). Mignolo adds that "the rhetoric of modernity and the logic of coloniality are…two sides of the same coin" (464), moving on to establish that "there is no modernity without coloniality" (Mignolo 466). While modernity claims the quality of bringing forth emancipation of sorts, Mignolo focuses on a darker side or a con aspect of modernity as being a "constant reproduction of coloniality" (450). The said reproduction addresses the beginning statement of this chapter about coloniality being subject to human relations, which are timeless and therefore not "stowed away in a black box" (Giddens 1). This is further confirmed by decolonial scholar Sabelo J. Ndlovu-Gatsheni, according to whom "[i]t is the continuation of colonial-like relations after the end of direct colonialism that has come to be termed as coloniality" (30). Since coloniality is integrally tethered to modernity and continually transpiring irrespective of time and space, —to phrase it in the words of Maldonado-Torres, "we breath[e] coloniality all the time and everyday" (243). It is not a surprise when Habermas exclaims that "the project of modernity has not yet been fulfilled" (12).[2] On that note, Quijano clarifies that "[i]f the concept of modernity…refers to the ideas of newness, the advanced, the rational-scientific, the secular, (which are the ideas normally associated with it) then there is no doubt that one must admit that it is a phenomenon possible in all cultures and historical epochs" (543).

The possibility, as mentioned above, hints at the numerous "non-Western concepts of Totality" (Mignolo 451) pitched against an "imperialist concept of Totality" (Mignolo 451)[3] which claims ultimate authority — "transmodern *pluriversality*" (Dussel 41) as against the imperial core. Mignolo elaborates how it is a postmodern (hence heavily Eurocentric) critique of this "Totality" (451–455) which leads to post-coloniality. In case the same analysis is implemented from the perspective of coloniality, it leads to decoloniality—which is a synthesis of "Quijano's project on *desprendimiento*" (Mignolo 452)[4] and Samir Amin's "economic de-linking" (435–444). Mignolo later used these concepts to develop his idea of "epistemic de-linking" (450). Since the clash of the multiple Totalities entails a power struggle with the economy as the basis of discrimination, Mignolo argues how Quijano's notion of "coloniality of power" (536) which embraces "world capitalism" (Quijano 536) and Eurocentrism, has two sides—the "analytic" (Mignolo 452), which affirms itself and the "programmatic" (Mignolo 452), which reacts to the analytic. To conclude, it may be said that "the analytic of coloniality and the programmatic of decoloniality moves away and beyond the postcolonial" (Mignolo 452). Thus, it is clear that the scope of resistance via decoloniality transcends the postcolonial. Taking the argument further, Ndlovu-Gatsheni expounds how "decoloniality is ranged against imperialism, colonialism, and coloniality as a constituent part of the modernist politics of dismemberment, alienation, exploitation, and alterity [and] attempts to make sense of what is happening, actually being faced, and being experienced, particularly from geopolitical sites that were the recipients of the negatives of modernity" (23–24). Thus, in narratives of decoloniality, these "geopolitical" sites (Gramsci 304) become the subject of deliberation and action, hence setting examples of staging "counter-hegemonic" resistance (Hunt 310).

Situating Orijit Sen's *River of Stories*

Indian graphic artist and designer Orijit Sen, in his first and only graphic novel, *River of Stories* (1994), reproduces one such geopolitical site, which presents itself as a breeding ground for economic and regional conflict and exploitation using the affordances of the comics medium. *RoS* is considered to be the first graphic novel in India which "opened the door for long-form comics work" (Stoll 329) in the country, despite the next graphic novel hitting the market almost a decade later with Sarnath Banerjee's *Corridor* (2004). *RoS* is the account of a reporter from the magazine *Voice* named Vishnu, who decides to cover the story of the Rewasagar Dam and the protests against its construction by the local villagers, urban and suburban activists, and tribal communities whose lands are at stake for the government project. However, there is a parallel narrative of a village singer who sings about creating the universe and the laws of humankind and animal-kind. The rural singer's tale stands in stark contrast to the world's western/rationalist/scientific history. It follows Vishnu from the comforts of his home in the city to a village named Ballanpur, where he seeks to excavate unheard stories about the protests against the building of the dam and as a journalist, writes an article that captures all the perspectives that he can garner in his time on the field. Thus, the text qualifies as expressive journalistic writing, albeit interspersed with history and local mythology. Mignolo's concept of Totality offers an exciting way of understanding the structure of *RoS* where it is safe to perceive the mythic voice of the village singer, Malgugayan, operating as one (perhaps the most significant) of the many silenced Totalities with the government officials playing the vocal Totality. The graphic novel is divided into three parts and an epilogue which marks the journey of a voice, initially unheard and speculative, gathering traction as it flows and then bursts out into the open world, thus transitioning from being "The Spring" (Sen 8) "The River" (Sen 29) to "The Sea" (Sen 50). Coincidentally, the medium through which the voice gets conveyed is a magazine named *Voice*! The first part constitutes the homework that Vishnu does before venturing out into the field. This again marks his knowledge or episteme of the issue at hand as extremely limited or stifled by the other voices and his dependency on them for a truth of the Totality he seeks. The second part throws him during the action, where the silent Totalities are audible, and the spring of episteme grows into a river of stories narrated on both ends of the stream—the local and the global. The third section is where the "programmatic" (Mignolo 452) union of the silenced Totalities lashes at the "analytic" (Mignolo 452) sea of vocal Totality and myriads of voices merge to create possibilities of decolonial resistance, reactions, and independent co-existence. However, this journey ends with realizing the silenced Totalities being finally heard and acknowledged begins with a problem.

The Problem

The problem is actualized by a rift in lifestyles between city-dwellers and bureaucrats on the one hand and village-folk and tribal communities on the other. The conflict takes on proportions of a politically, legally, and economically charged power struggle, which is undeniably the reproduction of coloniality. But under domestic circumstances, it is deprived of any imperialist urges, whose workings are manifested as soon as Vishnu commences interviewing his housemaid, Relku, for his story. When Vishnu questions Relku about her village, which happens to be Jamli, a place 3 kilometers away from Ballanpur and by the river Rewa (the recollection of this detail is crucial and will be discussed later), Relku narrates the story of how her family was evicted. They had to move towards the city to find work and shelter. This meta-narrative begins with an encounter between a government official and the members of Relku's tribe. As soon as the natives address the "*sarkaari*[5] people" (Sen 15) as "*sahib*"[6] (Sen 16), the discourse of coloniality is established and what ensues is that "[u]nder the spell of neo-liberalism and the magic of media promoting it, modernity and modernization, together with democracy, are being sold as a package trip to the promised land of happiness," (Mignolo 450) when the official lures the natives' imagination with promises of "*pucca*[7] roads," "proper means of transport," "proper houses," and "factories" (Sen 17). By the time the subject veers to their children receiving education and being intelligent, getting a job, and earning money as a reward, the natives believe all of this to be a joke and wonder, "how is it possible to live without farming or hunting?" (Sen 16) To the tribal communities, the very idea of such a Totality is inconceivable. As much as they are hesitant about the changes, they clearly would not mind, given no encroachment on their lifestyle. But little do they know that "[t]he outside of modernity is precisely that which has to be conquered, colonized, superseded and converted to the principles of progress and modernity" (Mignolo 462). Hence, the tribal people are meant to become targets of oppression and exploitation.

However, there are always a few who are either brave or foolish (giving adequate space to both parties concerned) enough to raise their voice and ask questions to which the bureaucratic administration responds by slamming "a crackdown on the more vocal ones" (Sen 21). Since it has to be clarified that "when people do not buy the package willingly or have other ideas of how economy and society should be organized, they become subject to all kinds of direct and indirect violence" (Mignolo 450); otherwise, there is a constant risk that if "the geography of reason shifts," (Mignolo 462) the entire system would be compromised. Reason and judgment belong to the economically and materially superior classes, and such parties would fain give up their position of comfort to create room for other minorities with credible voices. Subtle counter-measures, as a self-defense mechanism against the geographical shift of reason, act as snares for the less careful among the repressed — for instance, carving out areas of land and punishing those who trespass on it, marking those who skip providing gifts to the corrupt officials while revoking their permission to graze cattle, and in consequence constraining their freedom of movement, setting debt traps by selling alcohol on credit and countless other such maneuvers. Despite all the oppression, the officials' statement remains the same throughout — "All of you can benefit from these schemes, provided you learn to cooperate" (Sen 16) as if providing a choice, whereas there is no natural choice involved. This is how the "myth of modernity" (Mignolo 481) operates, being a "justification for genocidal violence" (Mignolo 482) behind the mask of emancipation. Coloniality, being the dark side or con of modernity, "exists as an embedded logic that enforces control, domination, and exploitation disguised in the language of salvation, progress, modernization, and being good for everyone" (Mignolo 6).

Relku's father, Antriyo, complains at the police station against Rathore Saab, the alcohol distributor, who encourages Antriyo's brother, Maaru, to drink as much as he wishes on credit thus ensnaring him in a debt trap. The police (bribed by Rathore) beat up Antriyo, who has no idea as to what wrong he did, and the next day Relku's house is set on fire while the entire family has to move to the city to work as "landless labourers...with no money or possessions" (Sen 28). It is a fact that violence is perpetrated. But, without the strictly colonial imperialist drive to conquer an area that is already on the brink of being evacuated by the inhabiting natives, how is violence being made possible at all? An answer to this question may be attempted by revisiting before the first encounter, where Relku is seen picking *mahua* flowers. At the same time, her brother, Somariyo, shoots an arrow and misses a bird — an idyllic image of the hunter-gatherer tradition (see Figure 1.1). The utopic atmosphere is ruptured with the sound of a motor engine. As soon as Somariyo (who is climbing the tree to fetch his arrow) notices the locomotive's sound, special attention is given by the author to the breaking of a branch and Somariyo falling through in-set panels. The tearing of the branch indicates what wa Thiong'o calls "dismemberment" (5) or the fragmentation of the self of a colonial subject. The sound of the motor engine is a clarion call to the imminent dismemberment of the natives and hence a moment of dramatic irony graphically represented. The dismemberment also breaks the being and sends the "*damnés*"[8] (Fanon 245) into a zone of "non-being" (Heidegger 177) where there is no face to show. "[T]he face speaks" (Levinas 87), and when it does, it "forbids us to kill" (Levinas 86). But when there is no face, there is meant to be violence, hence given the bureaucratic nature of the government officials, no one can be blamed, and how can one without a face accuse or be inculpated at all? The impossibility of what Levinas calls "face-to-face" (85) is, therefore, how violence is possible even without any spur or intent. Voice and visibility are markers that acknowledge the presence of a human being. Still, when the concerned human is deprived of both, there is a regression towards a sub-human stature where the choice of identity itself is snatched and controlled by materially developed humans, referring to the bureaucrats in the present context. They use the economy to claim mastery and control over the non-beings.

The comics' form, as seen above, not only visually represents a setting but situates and anticipates a time in a single frame. The comics form is known to be a reductive art form where the artist eliminates all redundancies until every scratch on the panel is significant in some way, thus providing novel artistic agency to the creator and, in the words of urban scholar Dominic Davies, becoming an engaging weapon in the hands of those residing and writing from the Global South. In his book *Urban Comics* (2019), Davies examines the comics of five southern cities—Cairo, Cape Town, New Orleans, Delhi, and Beirut—to argue that "comics are engaged with a range of decolonial projects" (Davies 4) and how comics are depicting the multiple divisive crises "in both their form and content with a radical revisioning of violent, neocolonial urban space" (Davies 4). Davies also quotes Orijit Sen calling himself an "infrastructural engineer" (Davies 181) who crafts his comics with panels, gutters, and all its attendant components just as a planner would design a city but can re-see and re-show the established structure by de-establishing it and re-inventing components. However, decolonial practices are not limited to cities and urban spaces alone. Sen's *RoS* is a solid testament to this contention as the same structures are being broken but in the backdrop of a rural grassroots movement.

Figure 1.1: Orijit Sen's *River of Stories* (14-15)

The Decolonial Stand

Given the decolonial potential of comics and perhaps because of the problems mentioned above, the text itself takes a stand in resistance to the coloniality/modernity framework. It does so by invoking visual aids that subtly indicate how the plot and the characters break the colonial/capitalist fabrications. The narrative allows both the ensnarling and the redemption of the *damnés* and relies primarily on four mighty pillars to initiate the decolonial movement that aims to negate completely and discard all foreign (here capitalist) influence—be it in thought, actions, or reactions. The first pillar of resistance is the mythical narrative of Malgugayan, with which the graphic novel begins. Instead of giving in to the rational/scientific/Western understanding of the world, *RoS*, while paying homage to the age-old tradition of oral storytelling, pays tribute to the local legend of the birth of the rivers Rewa and Vijali. The myth follows the story of creation "as believed in the Apa Tani tribe in Arunachal Pradesh" (Elwin 5). Although the action supposedly takes place by the banks of the river Narmada in Madhya Pradesh, Sen somehow links the two geographically distant and distinct cultures, fusing them into a singular force having roots in shared consciousness. Such a connection is meant to deal with heavy damage to the colonial stratagem of divisive policies that maim the ability of the repressed community to connect and heal.

According to the myth, before everything else, Kujum Chantu, a selfless mother figure who realizes that any movement she makes would mean catastrophe for the world to be. Hence, Kujum Chantu rubs the dirt on her chest to create life and sustenance for the life she creates and sacrifices herself so that the world may live. Sen's employment of a North-Eastern folktale in a narrative that is based in Central India is justified since multiple similar myths, where elementals procreate, or a sacrifice is made, can be found in various other cultures with different names—for instance, "*Phangnalomang* in the Dhammai tribe" (Elwin 13), "*Khupning-Kuam* in Singpho tribe" (Elwin 20–21), and the "myths of the Hrusso tribe" (Elwin 15) among others. The reader can hear the tale of Kujum Chantu through the songs of Malgugayan, who goes on to sing of how he came in possession of the *rangai* (the instrument he plays while singing). The yarn that follows is a digression from the creation story and assumes the proportion of an epic in the making, where Ranikajal sends Ratukamai to wake up the singer of *maal* (Malgu), who "sleeps for twelve years and snores for thirteen" (Sen 30) breaking all notions of western reason, and when called to the urgency of "our mountains are changing," responds "Go now, I will come after four-five days" (Sen 30). Malgu then sends a letter to Relukabadi, tasking him with making his instruments, who promptly goes across the mountains with his two daughters—Relu and Revli. The daughters were not meant to go with Relukabadi. Still, following the epic tradition, fate causes them to accompany him. By accident, both girls may become rivers (Ganga or Rewa and Jamna or Vijali) that flow freely throughout the land. Malgugayan delivers his instruments as promised. In this way, severe divergences are drawn between the local mythology, which views the resources and the life forms with a sustainable lens, and the rational/utilitarian opportunism, which draws on the false notion of development to hide the egocentric western vision of coloniality. Malgugayan symbolically also represents the dismembered self that stays behind, calling out to the other-selves lost amidst cityscapes hoping that "the river of stories which rises from the soul can flow out…to the far corners of the world, and people everywhere awaken to its sweet music" (Sen 31). The very existence of such a world at the backdrop, the beginning, and the end of the narrative is a bold statement of decolonial pride on the face of modernity/coloniality.

The second pillar of resistance is memory. According to wa Thiong'o, "[m]emory is the link between the past and the present, space and time, and it is the base of our dreams" (39). One of the primary agendas of the coloniality project is to uproot the memories so that they become nothing more than mere footnotes to be forgotten with time. As discussed before, dismemberment plays a significant role in this operation. The plot of Vishnu's journey starts with Relku's story about her childhood, and, as mentioned before, she recollects every detail about her childhood home and the harsh experiences that scarred her youth. Here, in the very beginning of the narrative, right after being introduced to the local myth of creation, the reader comes across a dismembered being in the process of remembering herself. Even before narrating her story, Relku is found singing a rural song, which is a point of connection with her mythic roots as the oral tradition is one of the primary sources of retaining memory and consequently music (which is the only weapon of resistance for Malgu) may be imagined as the cultural artifact that anchors myth to memory. When Vishnu reaches the village of Ballanpur, he meets Anand, an educated local activist involved in the protests against the construction of dams. He decides to join him and other protesters in the rally at Manigam to understand the other side of the story better. While on the bus journey towards Manigam, Vishnu and Anand chat about Malgu, the singer and evoke his memory in the hope that "[m]aybe this time Malgu's song will be heard not only by his people but by people all over the world," (Sen 43) all while Malgu is seen overlooking them from atop a mountain peak (see Figure 1.2). This frame is significant as two worldviews can be seen colliding and harmoniously celebrating an imminent victory of memory (that keeps a culture and a lifestyle alive) over indoctrination and subjugation.

Material Development and Human Regression 13

Figure 1.2: Orijit Sen's *River of Stories* (43)

The third pillar of resistance is the host of silent stories, which find a voice in the second part of *the River of Stories* titled "The River" (Sen 29–49). When Vishnu reaches Ballanpur and meets Anand, the readers showed an alternative side of modernity and development in the form of ecological awareness, sustainability, and humanitarian sentiments. Later, when Vishnu's eye-opening article is published in the magazine, particular focus is given on the face of the natives so that their voices do not simply remain random anonymous sounds but are graced with visible visages, showcasing human expressions, hence inculcating them with emotional value and authenticity. Thus, visibility and voice — which have been earlier stated as markers of "being" (Heidegger 22)— are returned to the bodies erstwhile rendered invisible and unheard, in the process attacking the integrity of the project of coloniality. On that note, the comics form uses the element of visuality to demonize the facial expressions of the oppressors like Rathore, the *sarkaari* people, and the police, while showing an empathetic side of the oppressed through mostly innocent and surprised or happy and scared faces with no scowl of malignancy on them (see Figure 1.3). This humanization of what Fanon calls "wretched sheep" (Fanon 232) is best made possible through the comics form as visuality is the primary approach of communicating sensitive concerns like human dignity and value for life.

Figure 1.3: Orijit Sen's River of Stories (22)

The fourth and most striking pillar of resistance is how Sen reproduces the topographical map of the Rewa valley, going beyond how a western cartographer would imagine the topography of an area of cultural as well as material significance. The map is drawn on a triple spread (therefore not possible to display as a single image) and covers the entire distance of the river Rewa to the dam site. Although it is not an accurate cartographic depiction with longitudes and latitudes, it shows a cultural and ecological perspective of understanding a landscape. The triple spread is also where the narrative plot and the mythic plot intersect and co-exist, thus creating sites of "pluriversality" through "border thinking" (Mignolo 498). That is to say, multiple totalities co-exist based on the premise of being marginal to the so-called capitalist mainstream Totality, hence nullifying the impact of the latter and creating individualistic and innovative codes of understanding physical space. This aspect is a fine example of a successful and straightforward attempt at decolonial thought and representation. Such re-imaginings of structured maps are exceedingly common among Indian graphic novelists and can also be found in Bhagwati Prasad and Amitabh Kumar's *Tinker. Solder. Tap. A Graphic Novel* (2009) where Delhi is visualized as a circuit board; or in Amruta Patil's *Kari* (2008), where a part of Mumbai is depicted as a hand-drawn dreamy carved-on-unplanned-lines sheet. Changing a topographical area in the mindscape becomes the first step of getting rid of the structures forced by colonial influence and aids in creating independent identities. Altogether, the four pillars stated above support Sen's graphic novel as an exercise in decoloniality with an eye out for breaking the chains of coloniality/modernity once and for all.

Coda: Under the Mahua Tree

The last section of *River of Stories* titled "Under the Mahua Tree" (Sen 57) is perhaps the most powerful in its critique of modernity and coloniality. A villager, who looks like Malgu, is playing his *rangai*,[9] sitting idly under a mahua tree. A helicopter "wups" (Sen 57) out of nowhere, and a stout person wearing a Nehru cap (clearly a politician figure) comes out and charges him for sitting idly. They have a short conversation where the administrator is emphatic that he should stop idling around and do some manual labor, which would earn him some money to afford luxuries, gain a profit, and then relax to enjoy the fruits of his work. Malgu, on the other hand, is disinterested and retorts sarcastically how that is what he was doing until the "noisy bird" (Sen 58) came along, destroying his peace. The bane of the Western reason is that it can only be applicable where reason is somehow forced. In a place where happiness and simplicity are considered more important than capital generation and wage against labor, logic does not have a place at all. Decoloniality strives to go out of the duality that reason offers and search for a third alternative that would suit its interest, irrespective of dependency. Speaking of other options, it is clear how comics, despite/because of being "a form once considered pure junk" (Chute 452), offers a potent amount of representation to a combination of both voice and visibility, thus proving to be ideal instruments of staging decoloniality and undoing the human regression perpetrated for the sake of material development.

Endnotes

[1] The italicization of "con" in "consequentiality" is meant to emphasize coloniality not only as a consequence of modernity but also as the 'con' of modernity, as will be discussed later.

[2] Although Habermas is concerned more with arts and aesthetics than economy and episteme.

[3] The idea of "Totality" used in this chapter relates to Walter Mignolo's concept of Totality.

[4] Loosely translated as "the act of detaching," from Spanish *desprender* (to detach) and – *iento* (the action of). In the words of Anibal Quijano, "[i]t is necessary to extricate oneself from the linkages between rationality/modernity and coloniality, first of all, and definitely from all power which is not constituted by free decisions made by free people" (Quijano 177).

[5] Hindi word for "Government."

[6] Hindi salutation to a respectable man of a better lifestyle than the speaker.

[7] Hindi word for "metalled."

[8] Fanon's "wretched" with an emphasis on the semantic connotations of the damned.

[9] A kind of flute.

Works Cited

Amin, Samir. *Delinking: Towards a Polycentric World.* Zed, 1990. Print.

Chute, Hilary. "Comics as Literature: Reading Graphic Narrative." *PMLA* 123.2 (2008): 452-65. Print.

Davies, Dominic. *Urban Comics: Infrastructure and the Global City in Contemporary Graphic Narratives.* Routledge, 2019. Print.

Dussel, Enrique. "Transmodernity and Interculturality: An Interpretation from the Perspective of Philosophy and Liberation." *TRANSMODERNITY: Journal of Peripheral Cultural Production of the Luso-Hispanic World* 1.3 (2012): 28-59. Print.

Elwin, Verrier. *Myths of the North-East Frontier of India.* Sree Saraswaty Press, 1958. Print.

Fanon, Frantz. *The Wretched of the Earth.* Grove, 2004. Print.

Faulkner, Willam. *Light in August.* Smith & Haas, 1932. Print.

Giddens, Anthony. *The Consequences of Modernity.* Polity, 1990. Print.

Gramsci, Antonio. *Selections from the Prison Notebooks.* Lawrence and Wishart, 1971. Print.

Habermas, Jürgen. "Modernity versus Postmodernity." *New German Critique* 22 (1981): 3-14. Print.

Heidegger, Martin. *Being and Time.* Trans. John Macquarrie and Edward Robinson. Blackwell, 1962. Print.

Horkheimer, Max. *Critical Theory: Selected Essays.* Continuum Publishers, 2002. Print.

Hunt, Alan. "Rights and Social Movements: Counter-Hegemonic Strategies." *Journal of Law and Society* 17.3 (1990): 309-28. Print.

Levinas, Emmanuel. *Ethics and Infinity: Conversations with Phillipe Nemo.* Duquesne University Press, 1995. Print.

Maldonado-Torres, Nelson. "On the Coloniality of Being." *Cultural Studies* 21.2 (2007): 240-70. Print.

Mignolo, Walter. "Delinking." *Cultural Studies* 21. 2 (2007): 449-514. Print.

Ndlovu-Gatsheni, Sabelo J. "Decoloniality in Africa: A Continuing Search for a New World Order." *The Australasian Review of African Studies* 36.2 (2015): 22-50. Print.

Quijano, Anibal. "Coloniality of Power, Eurocentrism, and Latin America." *Nepantla: Views from South* 1.3 (2000): 533-580. Print.

Sen, Orijit. *River of Stories*. Kalpavriksh, 1994. Print.

Stoll, Jeremy. "Indian Comics." *The Routledge Companion to Comics*. Routledge, 2020. 87-97. Print.

Thiong'o, Ngugi wa. *Decolonising the Mind: The Politics of Language in African Literature*. East African Educational, 1986. Print.

Chapter 2
A Tale of Things: Decoloniality of Memory in Orhan Pamuk's *The Museum of Innocence*

Chand Basha M
Department of Studies and Research in English,
VSK University, Bellary

Abstract

Museums are not only a physical space but also a symbolic space for generating, recreating and preserving memories. The patterns in which the wide array of objects is displayed in the museums evoke varied forms of social, cultural, political, racial, and other narratives. On a similar note, Orhan Pamuk's novel *The Museum of Innocence* plays a significant role in capturing the historical and cultural complexities of Istanbul, the capital city of Turkey. The city has been visited by different authors from different points of time, making Istanbul a socio-culturally intersectional space. But, due to various socio-political upheavals, the diverse memories have been systematically and epistemologically erased and narrowed down to certain specific cultural elements. These aspects further enhance the necessity of curating and preserving museums as sites of socio-historical memories. With the assistance of organizations like the EU and UNESCO, several museums in Turkey are being preserved in such a manner so that the museums can recreate the stories of different events and empires. On the basis of these arguments, through Pamuk's novel, this chapter reflects on the geopolitical memories of Istanbul, its cultural location, the Orientalist memories that are attributed to it, and the decolonial gestures.

Keywords: Museums, socio-political upheavals, Istanbul, events, Pamuk.

* * *

Introduction

The museum culture plays a significant role in defining Istanbul's historical and cultural complexity, a city located between East and West. The ambivalent setting of the city and the nation, i.e., Turkey, adds more significance to memories' cultures. The enigmatic metropolis evolves from Byzantium to New

Rome, then to Constantinople, to finally becoming Ottoman Istanbul. The city, frequented by various writers from East and West, has stocked the Ottoman memories, albeit it is an integral part of the new Turkey. The erasure of memories of different empires further makes preservation a significant trait of the Istanbul civilization. For instance, the modification of Aya Sofia, an epitome of the Byzantine architecture, into a Christian Cathedral, then into a mosque by the Ottomans, later into a museum in the era of modernity and a secular state, highlights the role played by museum culture in recalling the myriad civilizational encounters in Istanbul. Istanbul houses monuments that the archeological departments have preserved. With UNESCO and the EU providing monetary support to various preservation projects, today, Istanbul stands as a city of numerous monuments maintained well by various archeological departments. Many museums in Istanbul tell stories of different events and empires from the pages of history.

In this chapter, I intend to explore the geopolitical memory of the city and its cultural location in the era of globalization in Orhan Pamuk's novel *The Museum of Innocence* (2006). It addresses lived experiences on the edge of Europe, the orientalist perspectives attributed to it, and the decolonial gestures of Pamuk.

The novel *The Museum of Innocence* is a fictional representation of the actual museum, the Museum of Innocence, located in an ambivalent Istanbul—monumentally a western gateway of Asia. It is an eastern portal of Europe. Pamuk, who is also the metafictional character and the mouthpiece of the protagonist Kemal, narrates the tragic-romantic story of Kemal through artifacts stockpiled in the fictional (later actual) museum. It is also necessary to highlight the axiomatic proximity between the autobiographical being of the author and the creator of the museum in the novel. Kemal's meeting place with Füsun, i.e., the Mehmet Apartment, was a natural place where Pamuk, as he confesses in his memoir *Istanbul: Memories and the City*, met his unnamed beloved The Dark Rose. The protagonist of the novel did in the apartment what Pamuk did in his real life. At times, the biography of Pamuk and, at times, a fictional account of Kemal collide with each other adding autobiographical flavor to the novel. The author's fictional Kemal and the autobiographical presence or the autobiographical memories of Pamuk appear to contribute to each other's existence in many instances.

The novel narrates the desolate love of Kemal for his beloved Füsun and his stockpiling of artifacts connected to the personal meditation on his love, the past of Istanbul, and the cultures of people in Turkey. Each object collected by Kemal narrates a story about past events and people related to his beloved. While the fictional protagonist was stockpiling things touched by his beloved, the author simultaneously developed the actual museum in the Cukurcuma district of Istanbul. Besides writing a novel and setting an actual museum, Pamuk has also written a museum catalog, *The Innocence of Objects*, to activate a liveable interaction between the novel and the actual museum. While the museum of the fiction bespeaks stories of two beloveds of native Istanbul, the employment of western aesthetic frame, i.e., installation art, is used to translate material space into a space of narration. The non-fictional work supplies the intertextual, autobiographical, and historical trajectory of each object exhibited in the actual museum.

The vacuum created by the physical absence of Füsun is filled by the presence of her memories through the agency of objects which reap narrative power in the novel. Kemal stockpiles things and objects touched by his beloved. How do the stockpiled things keep the memories of the deceased beloved alive and make the life of Kemal happy? While mapping the fictional trajectory of objects, the things hence stockpiled also unveil a geo-cultural matrix of Istanbul and modernity in the Turkish social order. The meaning of ethnographic thickness appears to consolidate the argument that the suffering of being away from his beloved is overcome by the cultural and fetishist registers of objects.

The presence of the geo-cultural axis of objects in the museum is a significant proposition seen within the trajectory of decoloniality. The decoloniality of museums criticizes imperial museums and their archiving of colonial memories detached from geo-cultural locations of colonized societies. The museum culture has played a crucial role in understanding cultural practices, individuals, and geopolitical memories. The sites of the museum provide the history and social life of the bygone era to the present. The museum is a western invention. The space of the museum is a testimony of objects and monuments that became the subject of curiosity. The curiosity to know led the western explorers towards the new cultures of colonies. Things from the new world occupied the imperial museums. In his work *Postcolonial Studies: The Key Concepts*, Bill Ashcroft, Gareth Griffins, and Helen Tiffin engage with the trajectory of imperial museums thus:

> From the earliest days of European voyages, exotic minerals, artifacts, plants, and animals were brought back for display in private collections. Museums and live specimens were cultivated in the many private and public zoos established in the period. People of other cultures were also brought back to the European metropoles and were introduced in fashionable salons or traveled as popular entertainment. (77)

Some of the significant imperial museums that Pamuk, Walter D Mignolo, Ngugi wa Thiong'o, and Stephen Greenblatt refer to are The British Museum,

London; The Louvre Museum, Paris; the Berlin Museum, Berlin; and the State Jewish Museum, Prague.

The pressing issue with applying or understanding the Pamukian museum from the premises of decolonial thinking comes from Kemal's critical orientation towards museum and memory and their role in defining the essentials of cultural experiences. The novel critiques the act of memorization perceived by the discourse of Turkish ethnonationalism and European orientalism. Later the story re-orients the European museum model to suit the eastern sensibilities of Turkish society. The polemical co-existence of different ideas, otherwise considered binaries, in the novel provides a fresh look into dichotomies such as secular and religious, mystical and material, East and West. The story appears to create a space of negotiation through the intersecting zones between these binaries. In essence, mystical-material and secular-sacred elements supply critical essentials to looking at humanity beyond the eastern and western dichotomies.

I intend to map the genealogy of objects in the novel, where the authorities re-orient the museum model to tell the stories of the tragic-romantic love story of Kemal and locality. In the process, Pamuk does not discard the imperial or colonial legacy of the museum model. These stories further unfold various encounters between tradition and modernity, the secular and the sacred. The conflict between radical westernization and narrow provincialism and the state and the individual make a controversial presence in work. Pamuk's museum seems to take an epistemic departure from the colonial trajectory of the West to accommodate memories specific to the Turkish geo-cultural experience. The personal museum seeks a release from the logic of imperial museums, where the co-existence of the narratives of objects and their associated cultural feel is absent.

The Museum of Innocence and its mandate—verbalization of inanimate artifacts—can be seen as a site of multiple articulations of the East (the Ottoman past, Istanbul history, Sufism, the mystical, etc.) and the West (secularism, Western literature, the cultural materialism, etc.). Due to their symbiotic relationship, the novel and the museum are synonymously used in the chapter. The museum/novel enables polyphonic views in narrating contrapuntal memories of individuals like Kemal and Füsun, and broader worldviews associated with the interaction between western modernism and Turkish society in the 1970s.

The narrative imagination of the novel translates the museum into a chronotopic site. In *The Dialogic Imagination*, Mikhail Bakhtin discusses an "intrinsic interconnectedness of temporal and spatial relationship" (84) in constructing a particular world. Pamuk parallels the functions of a museum with that of the modern novel. The novel museum supplies contingencies of meaning to the lost essentials of the tragic story of Kemal. This tragic-romantic story bespeaks the modern time, i.e., the 1970s and the changing scenario of the city. A reader can discern the spatiotemporal importance, individual attachments, and associated relations with the objects in the actual and fictional museum. The museum and the novel are set within the spatio-temporal contours of modern Turkish society and Istanbul. At the same time, Kemal understands his museum as a place where one lives with the dead. Moreover, the museum is a place where time is transformed into space, the fusion between time and place is achieved.

Most importantly, Bill Brown uses the word "chronotope" (89) to refer to objects' spatial and temporal validity. While referring to Mason in his work *A Sense of Things*, Brown observes: "He [Mason] had come to believe that objects achieve significance not by being fit along a timeline but by being placed within a particular chronotope—historically embedded in a particular place, where they embed people in place" (89).

The chronotopic site helps construct narratives to build a cultural universe of the city. The novel narrates not only the city and the culture but also the lives of individuals that compose and form Turkish modernity and the culture of the town. Cultural presence and spatio-temporal relevance constellate person, place, and thing into an absorbing fiction, supposedly bringing a local culture of the city to life with the private memories of individuals as the connecting point of such an experience. These are the exhibits that insist that the meaning of things is disclosed by their function within a specific environment, which lends it a geo-cultural and chronotopic identity.

Artifacts as Contingencies to the Beingness of Beloved

> ...these fantasies were short-lived; before a day had passed, the old familiar suffering was again upon Apartments to take the cure. I would make straight for a teacup, a forgotten hair clip, a ruler, a comb, an eraser, a ballpoint pen—whatever talisman I could find of those blissful days when we [Kemal and Füsun] sat side by side, or I would rummage through the useless things that my mother had banished here [in the Mehmet Apartment], knowing that Füsun had touched or played with them all, leaving particles of her scent in incalculable measures. To find them was to see all the memories attached to each thing parade before my eyes, and so my collection loomed ever larger.
>
> (Pamuk, *The Museum* 178-179)

Memories of the lost beloved and the changing city are materialized through the stockpiled objects. The materialization of memory is different from cultural fetishism. Cultural fetishism is an orientalist project in which the displaced materials are used as a sign of information and a token of victory. The geo-cultural significance, historical trajectory, attached values, and stories are missing in the imperialist museums. Kemal avoids cultural fetishism in his act of materializing memory. While being detached from his beloved, Kemal tries to overcome the sense of loss and retain the mnemonic affiliation with his beloved through the objectification of temporality. The materiality of memory comes forth as he finds artifacts becoming the agency of his remembrance. Through these artifacts, he can recreate an affiliation with Füsun, separated from him first; she passes away later. The objects he stockpiles narrate three phases of existential predicaments Kemal goes through in the novel. The first phase of his romantic dilemma deals with his failed attempt to forget Füsun as he is engaged to his fiancée Sibel. In Füsun's absence, he finds artifacts to be the consolatory source for his agony. In the second phase, he becomes close to her family and succeeds in spending enough time with Füsun and her family members under various pretexts. He cannot accomplish a full-fledged intimacy with her as she marries Feridun halfway through the novel. During his pretentious visits to the Keskins (the family name of Füsun), Kemal steals objects touched by Füsun to overcome the gap between the two. The phenomenology of association between things and human beings can be discerned from his words: "Slipcovered armchairs, a table, a buffet holding a candy bowl, a set of crystal tumblers, and television crowned by a sleeping china dog—I found these things beautiful because they had all assisted in the making of the wondrous miracle that was Füsun" (*The Museum*162).

The third part of the novel narrates how he re-lives her memories in the aftermath of her death. The distance between the absence of Füsun, who is dead now, and the presence of her memories is bridged in the act of objectifying memory. In her absence, Kemal falls into the strange habit of taking consolation in objects. Kemal's act of stockpiling artifacts attempts to overcome the suffering of being away from his beloved. But Kemal does not overcome the loss of his beloved, a failure he is reluctant to accept even on the verge of his death.

The mnemonic affiliation with the actual museum and the material display of objects that appear in the 83 chapters of the novel has been verbalized in the story; hence, the book differs from the mere description of objects of imperial/oriental museums. The employment of ethnographic thickness escalates the poetic relationship between artifacts in the museum and stories in the novel. The novel supplies imagined historiography to each object in the actual museum. For instance, the thick description can be applied to understand the materiality of memories and their phenomenological role in defining the beingness of Füsun. Beingness refers to the essential qualities of Füsun's existence. For instance, the habit of collecting objects was triggered by his wish to relive the memories of his beloved. Kemal ascribes temporal and spatial contexts in which the objects were connected with her and the way they helped him recall Füsun.

From an anthropological understanding of the objects stockpiled by Kemal, we can see that the objects are, to some extent, de-territorialized from their original place without losing their essence. Kemal collects them from the Keskins and frees them from the domestic environment without erasing their spatiotemporal matrix and human context. While conferring on them a narrative value, Kemal transforms them into repositories of memories that unfold myriad associations, both personal and chronotopic, with Füsun and Istanbul of the 1970s. The denaturing of objects gives them a life of their own without altering their temporal and anthropological importance. The museumization of Kemal supplies an organic or animate role to objects. Things are translated into liveable narratives; Bill Brown observes similar phenomena in Strand's photographs, where objects are liberated from "their ontological status of being mere inanimate objects" (9).

An element of sensation is translated into a quality of things; spatial and temporal significance forms a thing. An object thus carries a certain amount of personal memories and conditions of history and socio-cultural experience. For instance, an object like the Jenny Colon bag functions as a testimony of individual experience. The associated value of the bag in the novel/museum signifies the "physical effort to overcome a metaphysical problem" (Brown 48). The metaphysical problem of Kemal indicates the longing for his beloved in her absence. Kemal perpetually relies on the material display of things, now ideas ascribed to objects, to exhibit his metaphysical problem—the loss of his beloved.

Objects assist him in finding with what Füsun was made. The earring, for instance, is a tale of lost essentials. It triggers memories of love and loss, generations of agony and unsuccessful love affairs, and a lover's longing for the beloved. Kemal's father triggers memories of his lost beloved through earrings, which bring the novel a materialistic rendering of spiritual hope and a physical display of metaphysical problems.

Footprints of Resonance and Wonder

I remembered that when I was a child, and my father came home from a trip, I would open this little suitcase and rummage through his things, savoring the scent of cologne and foreign countries. This suitcase was a familiar friend, a powerful reminder of my childhood, my past, but now

> I couldn't even touch it. Why? No doubt it was because of the mysterious weight of its contents.
>
> (Pamuk, *The Museum* 124)

A line of demarcation appears between mere description—containing temporal and spatial details of objects in a conventional museum—and the fictional narration, which carries a fictionally supported thick description of the museum. The imagined historiography in the fiction helps readers to access culture and knowledge, objects, and their journey across spatiotemporal borders and people who use them. Understanding the objects in the museum can be comprehensively discerned in the light of academic settings provided by Greenblatt in "Resonance and Wonder" (1990). The questions posed by Greenblatt pertain to the idea of resonance in defining my inquiry into the novel as well as the museum:

> A resonant exhibition often pulls the viewer away from the celebration of isolated objects and toward a series of implied, only half-visible relationships and questions: How did the objects come to be displayed? What is at stake in categorizing them as "museum quality?" How were they used initially? What cultural and material conditions made possible their production? What were the feelings of those who originally held the objects, cherished them, collected them, possessed them? (23)

The co-existence of the cultural matrix and the epistemic importance of the objects improve the understanding of the spatiality of the museum. Greenblatt's questions are framed within the spatiotemporal significance of the artifacts preserved in the State Jewish Museum in Prague. How do these objects in Pamuk's museum evoke exaltation in the viewer? How do the objects collaborate with the narrative matrix of the novel? What are the intertextual connections that make the objects livable? What are the different narratives and perspectives enforced on the objects in the actual museum? The correlation between the object and the novel adds to other intersectional subjects such as the autobiographical and fictional, real and surreal, verbal and visual in Pamuk's fiction.

While addressing these questions, I also clarify why memories of Kemal are contrapuntal. Each object in the museum does not hold a single story. Along with socio-cultural and spatio-temporal importance, the things tell multiple stories. For instance, the Jenny Colon bag plays the role of a referent for contrapuntal memories. While Kemal enters the Shanzelize boutique to buy the bag, he comes across his distant cousin Füsun, assistant shopkeeper. This bag indicates the starting point of a love affair between Kemal and Füsun, and its historicity, its derivation from the actress. She was adored by the French writer Gerard de Nerval. However, Nerval's love was never reciprocated, and subsequently, he committed suicide. Hence, the bag hints at a possible tragic end of the story of Kemal as well. The fictionality of objects cannot be suspended in their entirety as a mere act of imagination. This imagination also unfolds possible ways to render an imagined history and personal memories. The fictionality of objects in the novel explores the possible worlds of ordinary objects, which are otherwise ignored in the grand narratives of history and state-sponsored museums. The story opens up this possible worldview of every day or insignificant things of individuals, which can aptly be called imagined ethnographic thickness in Greenblatt's perspective.

The bag, first, in my view, is a reminder of the tragic life of the French novelist and his unaccomplished romantic affair with the actresses Jenny Colon. The genesis of the tragic romantic history embedded with the Jenny Colon bag indicates the sad end of Kemal. Pamuk's collaboration with the ethnographically charged Jenny Colon bag leads to the invention of narratives around the condition of vulgar distraction, a phrase Nerval uses in his *Aurelia* to indicate the bad memories of his beloved. The chapter entitled "Vulgar Distractions" in *The Museum of Innocence* shares intertextual connections with the tragic-romantic affair between Nerval and Jenny Colon and reinforces a similar relation between Kemal and Füsun.

The Jenny Colon bag, which is also available in a good number in the boutiques of Istanbul, unveils the trajectory of Eurocentric modernity imitated by modern Turkish society. The fakeness of the Jenny Colon bag signifies myriad interpretations: the eastern imitation of the West and the cultural fetishism prevalent in contemporary Turkish society; the blind model of West (Sibel alerts Kemal about the fakeness of the bag when he buys it for her) and crave for western goods and elite obsession with material culture. The quality of the object is a rhetorical reference to the proliferation of desire for western goods in Turkey. The object further stands witness to the presence of occidentalist fantasies among Turks in the 1970s. Hence, the bag in the museum serves multiple meanings, such as the possible tragic end of the fictional protagonist in the novel, the cultural receptions of Eurocentric modernity, and so on.

The objects in the museum pose pertinent questions about the usage of the same in our everyday life, meaning they create, qualities we ascribe to them, the role played by the attached values of objects in defining the beingness of fictional characters, and their role in framing a cultural image of the Turkish society. The things become repositories of anxieties, affections, attached values, fantasies, and memories.

The Synchronicity of Knowledge and Culture, and the Decoloniality of Museum

> Anyone remotely interested in the politics of civilization will be aware that museums are the repositories of those things from which Western Civilization derives its wealth of knowledge, allowing it to rule the world.
>
> (Pamuk, *The Museum* 71)

Pamuk seeks a correlation between lived realities and ideologies. In the present section, I intend to highlight Pamuk's project of bringing experience and knowledge, geo-cultural matrix, and objects into the singular space of a museum. Pamuk translates the narratives of a novel into an ideological representation of postcolonial subjects.

The epistemological combination of memory and museum has been a significant agency for the representation of postcolonial experience. The object-based recollection is often seen in a museum, which is originally a European concept. The imperial museums preserve the confiscated objects from the colonized societies; such artifacts are thus de-territorialized from their culture and environment in which they lived once. The decolonial thinkers disapprove of the orientalist representation of non-European or postcolonial cultures in the confined space of the imperial museums. However, they are not against the museum culture in particular. The cultures of human society are vibrant and liveable. Therefore, they cannot be understood only through the confined space of a museum, which appears to be a way of archiving cultures handpicked by the imperial establishments of the West. The problem lies mainly with considering the displayed objects as representatives of an enigmatic world order of colonized societies. Ngugi and Mignolo reiterate the misrepresentation of lived experience as a legitimate reason for the disapproval of the imperialist museum culture. The decolonial thinkers do not make a blatant denial of the museum; they call for the appropriation of the museum model to suit the socio-cultural logic of the east.

The metafictional characters in the novel unmask epistemological implications that befit the frame of decoloniality. The materiality and space of the Pamukian museum are defined not only from the perspective of structure of narrative aesthetics but also from an epistemological paradigm. A critical attempt is made to address the European perceptions of memory and its uncritical reflection on the experience of non-European cultures. In this regard, *The Museum of Innocence* serves two purposes: first, it critiques the western or imperial museum model and state-sponsored national museums in the east. Second, Pamuk proposes personal museums and city museums to see the social life of a city from the socio-cultural and chronotopic experience of an ordinary individual. A line of demarcation appears between two sorts of museums patronized by the state: personal/individual museums and national museums. There are also state-sponsored museums celebrating individual lives, such as Bronte Parsonage in Haworth, Anne Frank house in Amsterdam, Proust Museums in Paris, Nabokov Museum in Petersburg, and Brecht Haus Augsburg. Pamuk is not against the state-sponsored individual museums that reconstruct individuals such as thinkers and writers.

The protagonist in the novel leaves footprints of criticism that can be discerned parallel to decolonial thinkers. This criticism of space brings Pamuk, a writer from a residual area wedged between East and West, to an intersectional zone between the decoloniality of the museum and personal museums. Pamuk's ambivalent space is territorially and ideologically connected with neo-colonial conditions in modern secular nations. Hence, Ngugi wa Thiong'o's proposal for "globalectical reading" (72) helps us discern the nature of the novel. The concept of globalectical reading grapples with the shared problem with neo-colonialism in socially and culturally different spaces. Pamuk attempts to explore cultural memories outside the axis of the mere act of archiving or documentation enacted by the imperial museums of Europe. The above-quoted epigraph is an evident criticism of the protagonist towards the archive mania of the West. Intrinsically, Pamuk, as an author and metafictional character, creates the world's first synergetic novel museum.

The crux of this section relies on the differential nature of decolonial museums, as discussed by Mignolo in his polemical essay "Enacting the Archives and Decentering the Muses: The Museum of Islamic Art in Doha and Asian Civilizations Museum in Singapore" (2016). One of the essential natures of decolonization is the co-existence of knowledge accessed through objects in a museum and the learning culture. The museum, a site of education, and landscape, i.e., Istanbul, a place of experience, exist together in the scaffold of the Pamukian museum. The imperial museums archive the cultural memories of non-Europe and become a site of learning for the West. Decolonial thoughts disclose the limitation of the imperial museum and how they became a source of knowledge to European curiosity. The cultural environment of the archives in the imperial museums does not exist; because the artifacts are dislocated from their geo-cultural locations. Geo-cultural sites include territories, people, and the signature of the historiographic belongingness of the artifacts. The mere presence of objects cannot guarantee a full-fledged worldview of a cultural context and experience. But the literary association that Pamuk's museum shares with the novel appears to break the conventional modes of reading museums and novels. While the story supplies imagined historiography to objects in the actual museum, the real museum escapes the history of reality.

It recreates possible micro-narratives by sharing in integral literary association with the novel.

Why is it necessary to perceive the museum between the lines of the novel? The discernment of the imagined ethnographic thickness is supported by the laborious and garrulous narratives of Kemal. According to Kemal, a museum should not be an obituary to the deceased but "a place where one could live with the dead" (*The Museum* 503). The Museum of Innocence effectively invokes the fictional narrative of deceased Kemal. In his work *Orhan Pamuk, Secularism and Blasphemy*, Göknar aptly articulates the symbiotic correlation between the novel and the museum thus: "Pamuk is moving toward the central idea that novels, in their accumulation of things and creation of spaces of contemplation, are museums; and those museums, in their ordering and display of objects, are novels. Both social spaces are predicated on curating objects" (237).

Culture and experience define the spatiality and temporality of artifacts. According to the decolonial thinker, the East has a culture but not the knowledge of culture and modes of preserving culture within the framework of a western museum. This nuance gets a *bona fide* in Ngugi's reference to the body without mind and mind without the body mentioned in his path-breaking work *Decolonizing the Mind*. At this juncture of decoloniality of the museum, the words of Kemal critically call for a space of negotiation between the western model of the museum and cultural memories of the east. To fill an epistemological gap, Kemal calls upon the adaptation of the western museum model to the artistic sensibilities of the East: "What Turks should be viewing in their museums are not bad imitations of Western art but their own lives. Instead of displaying the Occidentalist fantasies of our rich, our museums should show us our own lives. My museum comprises the life I shared with Füsun, the totality of our experience" (*My Museum* 524-25).

The totality of his experience refers to world views perceived through an individual. The incident, on the one hand, refers to his affiliation with his beloved. On the other side, it relates to personal meditation on the testimonial changes in modern Turkish society. But the capitalist museum in the East and the imperial museum of the West fail to provide the totality of experience through objects. The novelist allows his protagonist to criticize the state-sponsored national museums that celebrate the nation's objects of great people of history or dynasties. The grand narratives of history ignore ordinary individuals and their magnanimous life. Pamuk makes the space of objects, i.e., a museum, a space of narratives. The tales of objects are supplied by the novel *The Museum of Innocence*. In reality, Kemal in the fictional world and Pamuk narrate the stories of individuals who constellate the geo-cultural memory of the city, i.e., Istanbul. It is also said that Istanbul does not have a city museum as such. *The Museum of Innocence* fills this gap of Istanbul not having a site of memories of the city. While the imperial museums, which Pamuk mentions in his interviews, are concerned with gathering information about other cultures and societies, the individual museum of Pamuk attempts to tell micro-narratives of individuals like Kemal and the city.

A parallel line of connection can be drawn between decolonial museums, as discussed by Mignolo, and personal/individual museums proposed by Pamuk. Pamuk seems to have a legitimate reason to criticize Imperial museums. While discussing his collaboration with Grant Gee's movie "The Innocence of Memories," in the article "Exhibition at the Pictures: Orhan Pamuk's Museum of Innocence on Screen" (2016), Pamuk declares the deconstructionist and postmodern epitome of personal narratives as opposed to the grand stories of the nation thus: "[T]he key to the future of museums is in our homes, in our daily lives, and on the streets. Museums should no longer concern themselves with history on a grand scale, the sagas of kings and heroes, or the forging of national identities; they should focus instead on the lives and belongings of ordinary people, just as modern novels do" (2).

Pamuk's museum takes a de-western stance while criticizing national museums and modern art museums of the east. Due to its ethnographic and socio-cultural relevance with the people of Istanbul, the personal museum of Pamuk/Kemal collaborates with the decoloniality of the museum. According to Mignolo, the act of de-westernization includes the proposition of not repeating the epistemic grammar of imperial museums which have preserved objects dislocated from their geo-cultural axis. Like those appearing in Mignolo's essay, Pamuk's museum holds artifacts of everyday life from the same locality. Contradicting the museums in Doha and Singapore, the objects in Pamuk's museum do not belong to the grand narratives of culture and art celebrated by kings and dynasties. These objects in the Pamukian museum do not belong to historically known people and distant places. The artifacts in the fictitiously real and realistically fictional museum belong to the people of the location instead of those of imperial museums. Pamuk appears to call for epistemic disobedience with Eurocentric aesthetics and exotic imperial museums. Simultaneously, the intellectual symmetry of his museum maintains an ideological distance from national museums in the east. Pamukian museum distinguishes itself from the matrix of power often exercised by the imperial museums and native museums celebrating native cultures at the grand scale of the nation. Hence, the assertion of his museum does not confine its edifices of criticism to decolonizing the western model of the museum. It steps ahead of, with a conceptual and epistemological collaboration with, decoloniality and proposes the personal museums different from those museums prerogative of monarchies in European and non-European contexts. The categorical museum, Pamuk suggests, is a non-imperial personal museum.

Pamuk appears to call for remodeling of museum frame in articulating the non-European cultures, hence delinking from the modes of representation cultivated by imperial museums of the West. To elaborate on the idea of epistemological departure from the western model of the museum, let me draw supportive propositions from Mignolo: "what is more, what is happening is not merely an imitation of westernization, but an enactment of de-westernization that western cultural standards are being appropriated and adapted to local or regional sensibilities, needs and visions. In the sphere of civilizations and museums, this is a significant departure" (4).

Mignolo makes these observations in the context of eastern museums in Doha and Singapore. Decoloniality of the museum does not propose eliminating museum culture from the axiomatic trajectory of the aesthetic and critical representation of cultures. According to the argument of decoloniality, the only option left is to transform the museum as a source of "story and as a space of narrative" (Mignolo 5), hence suspend the orientalist notion of seeing the eastern cultures as spectacle. The ideas of decoloniality and de-westernization of the museum are well-wrought in the context of Mignolo's observations on two museums in Doha and Singapore. The museums are located outside the European territories and see the sights of non-European cultures in a confined space of the museum. The assertion of decolonial museums, as Mignolo underscores in the context of museums mentioned above, is the appropriation of the western model and "the resurgence and re-emergence of civilizational stories that have been disavowed and arrogated by the very museum model being used" (6). But, the museums referred to by Mignolo are ironically supported by the hereditary monarchies craving for grand narratives of native cultures. Pamuk appears to criticize the ostentatious stories of native cultures as well. This subtlety between the decolonial museum and personal museum opens up another space of negotiation.

Works cited

Ashcroft, Bill, Gareth Griffiths and Helen Tiffin. *Postcolonial Studies: The Key Concepts*. Routledge, 2007. Print.

Bakhtin, Mikhail. *The Dialogic Imagination: Four Essays*. Ed. Michael Holquist. Trans. Caryl Emerson and Michael Holquist. University of Texas Press, 1981. Print.

Brown, Bill. *A Sense of Things: The Object Matter of American Literature*. The University of Chicago Press, 2003. Print.

Goknar, Erdag. *Orhan Pamuk, Secularism and Blasphemy: The Politics of the Turkish Novel*. Routledge, 2013. Print.

Greenblatt, Stephen. "Resonance and Wonder." *Bulletin of the American Academy of Arts and Sciences* 43.4 (1990): 11-34. Print.

Mignolo, Walter D. "Enacting the Archives and Decentering the Muses: The Museum of Islamic Art in Doha and the Asian Civilizations Museum in Singapore." *Ibraaz*, 6 Nov. 2013, www.ibraaz.org/essays/77.

Pamuk, Orhan. "Exhibition at the Pictures: Orhan Pamuk's Museum of Innocence on Screen." Trans. Ekin Oklap. *The Guardian*, 23 Jan. 2016, www.theguardian.com/books/2016/jan/23/exhibition-at-the-pictures-orhan-pamuks-museum-of-innocence-on-screen.

---. *The Museum of Innocence*. Abrams, 2006. Print.

Thiong'o, Ngugi wa. *Globalectics: Theory and the Politics of Knowing*. Columbia University Press, 2012. Print.

Chapter 3

Post-9/11, Cultural Amnesia and Representation(s) of Islamophobia in Ayad Akhtar's *Disgraced*

Abhisek Ghosal

Ph.D. Research Scholar,
Department of Humanities and Social Sciences,
Indian Institute of Technology,
Kharagpur

Abstract

Possessing Muslim identity in the post-9/11 United States is unquestionably a matter of potential risk, not only because of the dissemination of Islamophobic thoughts among the citizens of the US carried out by the ruling governmental authorities but also because of the intentional distortion of Islamic cultural traits. The post-9/11 terror strike has forced the US government to reconfigure the conventional relationship between West and East; it has built up counterterrorism squads to keep surveillance on the movements of both migrants and residents in the US and taken up a series of measures to beef up security at the border to execute the 'War on Terror' policy. Positional ambivalence of migrants in the US coupled with problems of insecurity leads them to put up transnational resistance to US governmental authorities. Posited against this context, Ayad Akhtar's *Disgraced* seeks to examine the intersecting trajectories among positional ambivalence, security and transnational resistance. This chapter intends to interrogate and deflate the efforts of Akhtar to build up postcolonial imaginary by means of transnational resistance in *Disgraced*.

Keywords: Positional Ambivalence, Securitization, Transnational Resistance, Post-Orientalism.

* * *

Introduction

The 9/11 terror strikes razed the Twin Towers and brought about a series of cultural and political alterations in America. Al Qaeda, an Islamic terrorist outfit, had been at loggerheads with American authorities over racial discrimination, cultural marginalization, and distortion of Islamic religiosity, among others, and carried out lethal airstrikes at Twin Towers, resulting in the escalation of political tension between America and Islamic organizations. America immediately resorted to several geopolitical and economic measures to provide security and safety to the American nationals and subsequently, declared war on terror policy to strike back at Islamic terrorist outfits. American governmental agencies began to distort Islamic identity and carried out massive crackdowns at different locations in America, thereby triggering Islamophobic thoughts in the minds of naïve American nationals. In response to America's war on terror policies accompanied by religious intolerance, Ayad Akhtar pens down *Disgraced* to deliberate on varied and questionable representation(s) of Islam conditioned by the cultural amnesia and post-9/11 geopolitical alterations. Thus, this chapter seeks to comment on Akhtar's critical interventions into the interface between cultural amnesia and Islamophobia in the post-9/11 scenario.

Historicizing 9/11: Its aftermath and the rise of Islamophobia

With the dissemination of neoliberal policies worldwide, followed by technological advancements, America began to express condescending attitudes regarding techno-commercial authority to developing nations, including Islamic countries. American government introduced significant changes in its foreign policies to expand its neo-colonial networks of exploitation. On the one hand, America put insistence on the implementation of neoliberal approaches to give a boost to the ailing economic conditions of developing nations and, on the other hand, was making attempts to intensify the tension between the West and the Rest of the world employing distortion and inferiorization of different sorts. Intrusive and aggressive economic policies of America, in a way, forced developing nations to yield to the economic ruses of America, thereby allowing privatization and transnational commercial enterprises to set in. In response to America's premeditated intrusions into the financial affairs of Islamic nation-states, Al Qaeda, an Islamic terrorist outfit, launched violent airstrikes at the Twin Towers on September 11 and shook America and the rest of the world. Immediately after the decimation of World Trade Centers, 9/11 got turned into a politico-cultural and historical signifier for future generations. 9/11, although primarily is a numerical referent, suddenly acquired historical and cultural significance after the fall of the Twin Towers. In other words, 9/11 turns out to be a politico-historical juncture where America's financial autonomy in pre-9/11 times and the rise of extreme dissensus politics in the garb of terrorism meet up. In the article "After 9/11—Thinking About the Global and Thinking About Postcolonial," Cameron McCarthy dwells upon how 9/11 redefines center-periphery problematic and exposes America's security gaps: "It is striking—with the intensification of representational technologies, mass migration, the movement of economic and cultural capital across national borders . . . how it is possible to send shock waves from the margins to the epicentres of modern life in the world we live in . . . ." (348). This temporal marker, that is, 9/11, freezes the pre-9/11 historical progression of America as an economic and technological supergiant and unfolds the politico-historical rewritings of the encounter between America and the rest of the world. For instance, President George W. Bush coined a few phrases to address the immediate aftermath of 9/11, and these phrases reflect how 9/11 impacted the reconstructions of political, social, and cultural discourses in America:

> in the aftermath of the attacks, the Bush Administration unquestionably generated an Orwellian litany of naming—a coalition of the willing, extraordinary rendition, war on terror, enhanced interrogation, regime change, preemptive war, homeland security —that has reshaped America's political discussion during the 2000s. (Duvall and Marzec 381)

Neil Leach is one particular critic who goes a step forward and argues that 9/11 did not only bring in radical changes in the restructuring of politico-cultural discourses but also left an impact on the psyche of American nationals. Leach puts it in "9/11" (name of an article): "I want to argue that the destruction of these towers has had a radical impact on the American psyche and that it is against the backdrop of the now absent twin towers that a new sense of American national identity seems to have been forged" (76). Rightly has Leach argued that decimation of the towers followed by psychological trepidations forced Americans to re-examine their national identities. It means that before 9/11, people of America used to forge their identities in terms of architectural establishments like the Twin Towers. After 9/11, they were forced to look up for some markers of their identity. When ordinary people of America got engaged in exploring some features of their identity, the 9/11 Commission Report was then brought in public to affirm that the American government was steadfast to restore its national integrity and glory and plan to execute strategies and recommendations suggested in the Commission Report. For instance, it is indicated in the Commission Report that the American government needed to focus on ". . . how to organize the White House staff, to the stepped-up investigation of and immigration enforcement against Muslim aliens, to the early diplomatic and military plans for dealing with Al-Qaida's sanctuary in Afghanistan" (Falkenrath 178). It points out that 9/11 overtly exposed loopholes in America's foreign policies and internal political affairs and insisted that serious and adequate attention was required to "the subject of the border and transportation security" (Falkenrath 184). It suggests that 9/11 altered

America's outlook to the rest of the world and ". . . FBI's authority to collect information on suspected and potential threats was enhanced shortly after 9/11 by the USA Patriot Act. . ." (Falkenrath 185). The FBI's authority was immediately augmented to detain illicit Muslim migrants in America and subsequently use them as spies to keep watch on the movements of the Muslim communities. It clearly explains how slowly but surely, massive raids by the FBI and other Intelligence agencies at different pockets and corners in America fueled Islamophobic thoughts among ordinary people. As Islamophobic views were brewing up in the minds of Americans, Islamophobia was brought in the State policy to devise political and administrative strategies to foil terrorist attacks further. The US officials began to keep an eye on Muslim people assuming that naïve Muslim people can critique terrorist activities committed by Muslim radicals. In *The Muslim World after 9/11*, Angel M. Rabasa et al. pertinently observe: "It is fundamentally difficult for non-Muslims to influence the perceptions of Muslims about their religion. Only Muslims themselves have the credibility to challenge the misuse of Islam by radicals" (4). It means that the US officials were intently looking for Muslim loyalists who would dissuade Muslim radicals from being brainwashed by terrorism. At this point, one may stop and think: was 9/11 an American event? Were the US security personnel kind enough to naïve Muslims while carrying out raids? 9/11 was neither an American nor an Islamic event but has had political bearings on the historical rewritings of the struggles of developing nations against the condescending attitudes of the US. In other words, 9/11 cannot only be examined as an exemplification of terrorism but a politico-historical rupture that disrupted the US' steady techno-economic advancements across the world. The US authorities were not kind to Muslim immigrants living in America simply because they interpreted Islam as equal to terrorism and mobilized non-Muslim immigrants and locals against American Muslims. Angel M. Rabasa et al. thus cogently observed:

> September 11 opened a new era in the United States and Europe, but not in the Muslim world. Most Muslims were horrified by the death and destruction wreaked by the September 11 attacks, but many—particularly in the Arab world—found some satisfaction in the idea that America's nose had been bloodied and that the United States had felt some of the pain that they believed had been inflicted on Muslims. So condemnation of the attacks was common but conditional. (50)

It seems that Muslims living in different Islamic nations were tacitly extending support to those who had attacked the towers. Therefore, US officials stepped up military and security measures to withstand further attacks. They began to apprehend that Islamic terrorist outfits might carry out deadlier attacks on the

US because the US was revising its political and economic policies. It can be argued that US security agencies started to pay intense attention to American Muslims who could shield the citizens of the US. It once again attests that US authorities were stepping up security installations to take on the challenge of Islamic terror outfits. In the article "Combating Islamophobia," Douglas M. Johnston points out:

> From a strategic point of view, American Muslims constitute one of our more formidable assets in the global war against militant Islam. Not only have they been instrumental in uncovering a significant number of Al-Qaeda plots against the US, but they also enjoy extensive influence with Muslim communities overseas that could be usefully engaged to good advantage, many in places of strategic consequence to the US. (171-172)

So, it is clear that US authorities resorted to an aggressive strategy like this one: Muslims in favor of the US. Besides, the US could not take decisive steps to end Islamophobia; rather, it expedited the rise of Islamophobia by otherizing Muslims in particular. In other words, on the one hand, US authorities paved the way for Islamophobic thoughts to rule the roost and, on the other hand, took it as an opportunity to otherize Muslims. In the article "Negotiating Muslim Youth Identity in a Post-9/11 World," Cynthia White Tindongan remarks: "The attack provided a serviceable kind of knowledge that fed into Islamophobic hysteria and precipitated the war on terror and wars against two nation-states. It created a convenient opportunity for Othering Muslims and has conflated Islam with fundamentalist Islamic movements and terrorism" (81).

Taking recourse to this critical observation, one may argue that the US' exploitation of Muslims as potential spies needs to be critiqued, for US authorities, on moral grounds, are not supposed to put naïve American Muslims in jeopardy. In other words, no particular religion, be it, Islam or Christian, can be associated with terrorism since no religion preaches its devotees to follow the path of terrorism. But, the use of Muslims as spies to get more robust intelligence by US officials leads postcolonial critics to frame the charge of racism against them. To defend Islamic terrorist outfits, the US launched state-sponsored violence against Muslims based on the mere suspicion that some Muslims living in the US had proximity to terror outfits and were thus potential threats to the US. But, unfortunately, in the name of raids, the US had made Islamophobia appear worse than ever. Miriam F. Elman is a vital critic who contends in "Islamophobia" (name of an article): "Islamophobia has traditionally been defined as both a prejudice and hostility toward Muslims that manifests as a distorted simplification of Islam and the Muslim world and as an irrational hatred, alarmism, dread and fear of the faith and its followers" (146). But in the post-9/11 context, Islamophobia got a new dimension: threats of otherization. Elman rightly argues that in the post-9/11 scenario, anti-Muslim thoughts were intentionally institutionalized to discriminate against Muslims as a religious minority in the US. Thus, they were time and again subjected to humiliation, torture, and torment. To substantiate Elman's observation, one may readily refer to Amartya Sen's insight in *Identity and Violence*, where Sen has extensively dealt with the threats of the prioritization of one identity over another and singularization of identity: "Violence is fomented by the imposition of singular and belligerent identities on gullible people, championed by a proficient artisan of terror" (2). It means to imply that no particular identity could be taken as "the person's only identity" (Sen 5). However, the US authorities forced select Muslim youths to spy on their neighbors under tremendous threats of incarceration and physical assault and subsequently to provide tip-offs to concerned security personnel. In this way, the US triggered Islamophobic thoughts in the minds of Muslims and non-Muslims alike.

Politics of Cultural Amnesia and Epistemic Endosmosis

Simply speaking, cultural amnesia refers to the forgetfulness of one's cultural associations. In other words, if one suffers from cultural amnesia, it is assumed that the person has forgotten the roots, customs, morale, cultural traditions, which used to be followed by him. In a seminal book titled *Belated Travelers: Orientalism in the Age of Cultural Dissolution*, Ali Behdad has extensively dwelled upon "the micropolitics of Europe's desire for the Other" (2), for orientalist discourses, are only counter-hegemonic but also speak of the formative and productive power of other in colonial discourses. Behdad has meant to say that postcolonial critics are belated travelers who engage themselves in exploring the constructive and effective potentials in colonial discourses. They attempt to retrieve the glorious past of colonized people, contested and replaced by the colonizers' culture. In the view of Behdad, the anamnestic retrieval of the past is a political event that is contingent upon one's power of recognition.

In fact, in "Amnesia: Cultural Memory, Reconciliation, and Communal Accountability in the Americas," Lessie Jo Frazier cogently comments: ". . . [the] politics of cultural amnesia entails more than its common association with repression, editing, or erasure, being more complex than other terms current in memory studies: forgetting, silencing, and denial" (147). According to Frazier, the politics of cultural amnesia is more complex than Memory studies, for the former is premised on the intricate interactions between repression and erasure conditioned by the exercise of power. Cultural amnesia ". . . entails the slippage between, on the one hand, public attributions of memory loss and accountability for a given person and the consequent collective assumption of a gap whereby we accept that access to past events has been lost, on the other" (147). It is understood to be a slippage that can be located in between memory loss and a gap. Fluidity and transformability of amnesia in compliance with cultural alterations are worth considering because they can lead one to understand how the politics of cultural amnesia is played at praxis. Instead of viewing cultural amnesia as regressive and unpromising mental space, Frazier persuasively contends: ". . . amnesia did facilitate the possibility for some sort of workable future of interaction not through attempting an explanatory continuity of past, present, and future, but rather through framing a silence, an implicit recognition of an incommensurable difference and unrecuperable past" (158). It suggests that one has to accept that the politics of amnesia is grounded on an implicit recognition of an incommensurable difference and unrecuperable past and therefore is very useful in understanding West's micro-political desires for orientalist discourses.

In the context of the US' retaliatory moves against naïve Muslim citizens dwelling in different parts of the US, resistive discourses can be considered to comment on America's aggressive retaliation. Induced by global connectivity in terms of technology and transport system, it has become easier for the US to circulate Islamophobic thoughts among people worldwide. Hamid Dabashi is one particular critic who has coined the term epistemic endosmosis to elucidate how West indulges in the warped representation of Islamic cultural ethos in *Post-Orientalism: Knowledge and Power in the Time of Terror* (2009):

> *epistemic endosmosis,* namely a phase in the post-Orientalist period when such knowledge is no longer centered in any university or research institute and is widely disseminated in varied forms of private and public forums, and as such resisting categorization and operating on a cacophonous modulation. *Endosmosis* here refers to the inward flow of dis/information through the permeable membrane of the mass media—a cellular labyrinth of dissemination or cavities of transmutation—toward the public domain at large and there mutated into a greater concentration. (222)

Dabashi is quite right when he says that instead of constructing docile subjects, the West promotes warped knowledge regarding terrorism using social media, which, unlike other popular media, can unite people of diverse races, cultures, classes, nations, to name only a few, to exhibit its epistemic condescension. What is striking is that the West ingeniously attempts to leave an impact on a mass scale by disseminating power. Dabashi has rightly argued that the site of production and dissemination of knowledge, in the post-9/11 context, turns out to be a site of resistance at praxis. In other words, it can be contended that the US' efforts to spread misinformation regarding religious traditions in Islam have to be countered employing anamnestic retrieval of the past. Religious ethos in Islam needs to be brought up to refute the following myopic observation on the US authority that Islam backs up terrorism and is thus vicious to the political, social, and cultural securities.

Akhtar's *Disgraced* and Representational Politics

Ayad Akhtar carves out a substantial niche for himself in the arena of South Asian literature by penning down some riveting dramas on various emerging issues. Akhtar's literary corpus comprises *Disgraced* (2013), *The Who and The What* (2014), *The Invisible Hand* (2015), *Junk: The Golden Age of Debt* (2016), *American Dervish* (2012), among others. In *Disgraced*, Akhtar has delved deeper into the process of stereotyping Muslim citizens living in the US after the 9/11 terror strike as potential dangers to the security of the nation. This drama features Amir, a forty-year-old Muslim of South Asian origin, and Emily, a thirty-year-old American. Both of them occupy the central positions in the drama, and their actions contribute to the making of the plot. Interactions between Amir and Emily divulge how stereotyping Muslims as potential risks at socio-cultural status quo in the US are intently done. It also reveals how conventional perceptions of the Orient are torn up into pieces by Emily, who finds interest in Islamic cultural practices despite being a citizen of America. Opposed to Emily, Amir wants to cast off his Muslim identity to get over the sudden and furious raids of the US government. Amir, a public prosecutor by profession, refuses to advocate for Imam Fareed, who is suspiciously accused of being a potential terrorist for running a mosque. Amir is apprehensive of agential raids and is overtly critical of Islamic cultural practices. By contrast, Emily brings out the beauty in Islamic art to imply that it is unwise and unfair to equalize Islam with terrorism simply because radicalized persons often misconstrue Islamic ethos. Apart from it, the precious inputs of Abe and Isaac, in the middle, make the interactions between Amir and Emily more interesting. Towards the end of the play, both Amir and Emily can comprehend each other. The playwright attempts to bridge the gap between seemingly contrary views about Islam, which Amir and Emily perform.

In an interview, while responding to the representation of the Muslims in the play, Akhtar said: ". . . [the] play begins with a Western consciousness representing a Muslim subject. The play ends with the Muslim subject observing the fruits of that representation" (96). This observation reflects how oriental discourses concerning Islam have been pervasive throughout the play. Representational politics has been a central issue that governs the movements and conversations of all the characters featured in it. When the play opens, readers are introduced to a large painting that hangs down on the wall and is a constant reminder of an Islamic garden. The impressive and expensive décor of the protagonists' living room reflects how Islamic cultural values are still celebrated in post-9/11 America. It also gives the impression that protagonists are engrossed in Islamic religious traditions and enjoy the lustrous and magnetic repercussions of that painting. Opposed to this elaborate stage paraphernalia, Akhtar has shown the various ways through which the issue of name changing becomes imperative for those who are scared of their Muslim identities. Amir happens to be one of the many Muslims who, despite having a decent social standing, looks frightened of his own Muslim identity because, in the post-9/11 scenario, US security agencies exploited state power to intrude on their lives. While having a chat with Emily, Amir said: ". . . [I] had my Social Security number changed. When I changed my name" (Akhtar 36). It shows that Amir yields to the discourses of Islamophobia which operates through epistemic endosmosis, thereby affecting ordinary people, including Muslims in the US. In other words, the US authority chooses to represent Muslim people and deliberately misconstrue Islamic cultural values to take revenge against the people of Islam in general.

Interestingly, Amir fails to resist the US epistemic politics and ends up being prey to it. One may cite another textual instance to corroborate how Islamophobia regulates the actions and thoughts of Amir. At one point in the drama, Amir says:

Amir: It's a nightmare at the airports.

Jory: And now there's a whole new attraction.

. . .

Amir: On top of people being more and more afraid of folks who look like me, we end up being resented, too. (Akhtar 49)

It reveals the grim reality that people looking like Amir resent their Muslim identities and live with dire apprehensions. What is even more significant is that Islamophobia leaves an indelible impact on the minds of immigrant Muslims who detest Islam only to evade the glaring eyes of US authority. Amir speaks out: ". . . I don't see eye on eye on Islam. I think it's . . . a backward way of thinking. And being" (Akhtar 52). At this point, one may stop and think: does Amir detest his own Muslim identity, or is he forced to comply with the Islamophobic discourses perpetuated by US officials? To expose the psyche of Amir, one may refer to the following conversation:

Isaac: Did you feel pride on September 11?

Amir (With hesitation): If I'm honest, yes.

> Emily: You don't really mean that. Amir.
>
> Amir: I was horrified by it, okay? Absolutely horrified.
>
> Jory: Pride about what?
>
> > About the towers coming down?
> >
> > About people getting killed?
>
> Amir: that we were finally winning. (Akhtar 62-63)

This conversation is connotative because although Amir overtly slates Islam, he willy-nilly supports terror strikes in America, possibly because it gives him a sense of collective retaliation. It also insinuates that Amir, under tremendous psychological pressure forged by the discursive practices of Islamophobia, criticizes his own Muslim identity. Amir intentionally (mis)represents his religion only to prove his loyalty to US authority. In a way, Amir indulges in disseminating anti-Muslim sentiments among others to evade possible arrest. On the other hand, US officials use native Muslims like Amir to keep an eye on the Muslim community and to convince non-Muslim immigrants about the vicious nature of Islam.

Akhtar has possibly incorporated the character of Emily not only as a foil to Amir but also as a rebel who questions the viability and integrity of Islamophobia by critiquing cultural amnesia. In a way, Emily takes US authority to task for spreading Islamophobic thoughts among US nationals and being a non-Muslim America; she brings up rich cultural values embedded in Islam through practicing anamnestic retrieval of the past:

> Emily: The Islamic tiling tradition, Isaac? Is a doorway to the most extraordinary freedom….in my case, of course, it's not submission to Islam but to the formal language. The pattern. The repetition. And the quiet that this work requires of me? It's extraordinary.
>
> Emily: The Islamic tradition's been doing it for a thousand years. Pardon me for thinking they may have a better handle on it. (Akhtar 31)

Despite being white, Emily shows considerable interest in Islamic art and cultural ethos. What Emily subtly does is that she deflates parochial oriental discourses, which undermine the values of Islam. Just as the US uses Amir to speak in favor of the US standpoint, Emily writes back at the US to excavate the forgotten past of Islamic culture. One may refer to another essential dialogic interaction between Emily and Isaac, which reflects powerful observation and ratiocination of Emily:

Isaac: Islam is rich and universal.

. . .

Emily: The Renaissance is when we turned away from something bigger than ourselves.

. . .

Isaac: Right.

Emily: That never happened in the Islamic tradition. It's still more connected to a wider, less personal perspective. (Akhtar 47)

Emily, unlike Amir, decodes the US' politics of cultural amnesia and thus tries to put up counter-discursive resistance by deliberating on the cultural and artistic significance of Islam. At this juncture, one may stop and think: does Amir subscribe to Emily's viewpoint on Islam or stand as a foil to her? At one point in the drama, Amir confides in Emily: "To be Muslim—truly—means not only that you believe all this. It means you fight for it, too" (Akhtar 62). It shows that Emily can influence Amir's thoughts on Islam and pushes other characters to speak up against the myopic representation of the Orient. For instance, Abe is one character who lashes out Western views on Orient: "For three hundred years they've been taking our land, drawing new borders, replacing our laws, asking us to want to be like them. . . . They disgraced us" (Akhtar 85). This expression attests to the fact that characters other than Emily gradually understand the importance of epistemic retaliation by adhering to Islamic cultural ethos.

There is a point in the drama when Emily overtly takes on US authority's support for Islamophobia and surveillance: "About me being a white woman with no right to be using Islamic forms?" (Akhtar 29). It clarifies Emily's stern stand against epistemic violence perpetrated by US officials. What is significant is that racism has been operating at the backdrop and is subtly twisted with Islamophobic thoughts. The appearance of a Muslim immigrant is often suspected of causing an escalation of anxiety over his stay in the US. The incorporation of Emily in the drama is meant to rewrite the US' attitude to Islam and invigorate Muslim immigrants to take on flawed representation(s) of Islamic identity by the US authority. Towards the end of the drama, Amir admits: "I'm finally seeing what you were seeing. I'm finally understating your work" (Akhtar 86). This realization of Amir certainly vouches for Emily's relentless efforts to deflate the politics of cultural amnesia and epistemic violence by the US.

Conclusion

Ayad Akhtar's *Disgraced* ultimately turns out to be a harangue on Islamophobic discourses sponsored and propagated by the US authorities and innocent Muslim immigrants, respectively. Akhtar has taken up representational politics when the US launches a war on terror policy and puts cultural amnesia at work. Thus, choosing Emily in contrast with Amir happens to be a calculated move on the author's part, which puts forward that anamnestic retrieval of Islamic art is needed to ruin Islamophobic discourses. To explain this contention, one may refer to the ending of the play when Amir comes across a painting based on Velazquez's Moor and sketched by Emily and he "takes a searching long look" (Akhtar 87). This gestural change in Amir discloses the fact that Amir ponders over Islamic art and culture reflected through the painting. In a way, Emily's painting revives Amir's interests in Islamic art and culture, and it certainly upsets US' representational politics.

Works Cited

Akhtar, Ayad. *Disgraced.* Back Bay Books, 2013. Print.

Behdad, Ali. *Belated Travelers: Orientalism in the Age of Cultural Dissolution.* Duke University Press, 1994. Print.

Dabashi, Hamid. *Post-Orientalism: Knowledge and Power in the Time of Terror.* Transaction Publishers, 2009. Print.

Duvall, John N., and Robert P. Marzec. "Narrating 9/11." *MFS Modern Fiction Studies* 57.3 (2011): 381-400. Print.

Elman, Miriam F. "Islamophobia." *Israel Studies* 24.2 (2019): 144-156. Print.

Falkenrath, Richard A. "The 9/11 Commission Report." *International Security* 29.3 (2004/05): 170-190. Print.

Frazier, Lessie Jo. "Amnesia: Cultural Memory, Reconciliation, and Communal Accountability in the Americas." *Comparative American Studies: An International Journal* 13.3 (2015): 146-160. Print.

Johnston, Douglas M. "Combating Islamophobia." *Journal of Ecumenical Studies* 51.2 (2016): 165-173. Print.

Leach, Neil. "9/11." *Diacritics* 33.3/4 (2003): 75-92. Print.

McCarthy, Cameron. "After 9/11—Thinking About the Global and Thinking About Postcolonial." *Cultural Studies* 2.3 (2002): 348-353. Print.

Rabasa, Angel M., et al. *The Muslim World after 9/11.* Rand Corporation, 2004. Print.

Sen, Amartya. *Identity and violence: The Illusion of Destiny.* Penguin Books, 2006. Print.

Tindongan, Cynthia White. "Negotiating Muslim Youth Identity in a Post-9/11 World." *The High School Journal* 95.1 (2011): 72-87. Print.

Chapter 4

Ancient Stories, Current Praxes: Decolonial Myths in Contemporary Literature

Feroza Jussawalla
Professor Emerita of English,
University of New Mexico

Abstract

A new and popular horror film entitled La Llorona has captured the American audience. It tells the story well known to most US residents of Hispanic heritage, of a crying woman who emerges from rivers and lakes to capture children. In (re)telling this story, the hope, I think, of the producers is to tell the story of the colonial heritage of the Hispanic peoples of the Americas. There are two intertwined myths that have made their way into the American literary imagination. The original story of La Llorona is told in a novella by the father of Chicano literature, Rudolfo Anaya. Re-telling these myths as stories of colonization and decolonizing has long been part of the literature of the Western US. This task was even taken up by D.H. Lawrence as he confronted and contested prejudice towards the Native Americans and rewrote the story of Quetzalcoatl in two novels. This chapter studies the texts and the place of these myths in the task of decolonizing the Western American imagination.

Keywords: La Llorona, Hispanic heritage, intertwined myths, Chicano literature, Western US.

* * *

Introduction

Since myths tell the local stories of a culture's heroes and heroines, including that of indigenous peoples' oral histories and stories, in the telling of and retaining of these stories, they hold identity and, in that itself, are immediately both decolonial, because they capture the moment of contact and the gap at that moment, and decolonizing, because, they awaken the consciousness both in the past and present of oppression and suppression. Decolonial myths tell the stories of the moment of a culture's interaction with either a colonizing power or a settlers' situation. Mignolo and Walsh define decoloniality as an interconnection, between cultures coming into contact, rather than as the actual historical process of "decolonization" or getting free from the colonizer (25). For them, decoloniality is a praxis (a practice), not a strategy. Decolonization, on the other hand, is both a historical and cultural process. In some ways, this distinction is similar to Aijaz Ahmed's difference between post-colonial and Postcolonial, where Ahmed, while critiquing Said, asks for more attention to the specific historical moment of postcoloniality, i.e., when independence (and Partition, which he calls our fault), from "a colonizing power, actually happened, as opposed to the more metaphoric idea or concept of postcoloniality or freedom from the ideas and culture, of imperial rule, as we understand it today" (34). Mishra and Hodge pick up on this idea of Ahmed's in their now-famous review of Ashcroft, Griffiths, and Tiffin's *Empire Writes Back* (1989) by distinguishing between postcolonial with a hyphen and without. In times of cultural struggle to recall the histories of cultural contact and the power struggle, a return to the myths a culture has carried with them is always a decolonizing effort.

The notion of decolonization is different from how Mignolo and Walsh see decoloniality. Decolonization, of course, stems from the long, almost forty-year history of the process of postcolonialism. The word postcolonial was first used by Senator Daniel Patrick Moynihan in the 1960s when he sought aid for the countries which had just gained their independence from Britain. The development of postcolonial studies can perhaps be attributed to the first publication of *Orientalism* by Edward Said in 1978. Orientalism has been much contested, first by British historian Robert Irwin and then by Bernard Lewis. He chose to present the Jewish objections to Said's critique of the West.

Indeed, while the work of the triumvirate of so-called postcolonial theory – Said, Spivak, and Bhabha is essential here, it is also important to acknowledge their indebtedness to European thinkers and thought processes. Is this, therefore, indeed a decolonized theory? While each has coined a term that is now part of our critical discourse terminology, the words like Orientalism, Subaltern, and Hybridity all look westward. They are, therefore, to me, not so valuable for a decolonizing project. While Said criticizes the so-called "superior Western knowledge and power" (244) throughout his book *Orientalism*, his research looks to Western scholars, notably Marx. A simple look at Marx's article "British Rule in India" shows him to be probably the most racist towards the religion and peoples of what he called "Hindoostan" (14).

It would, however, be wrong to say that the notion of postcoloniality was developed by and through the work of these American based academics at prestigious and wealthy ivy league universities, any objection that can be levelled at Said, Bhabha, and Spivak, all of whose work also rely mainly on Western and European, sometimes Marxist theorists, Marx and Althusser, but largely Heidegger, Hegel, Foucault. The real work of decolonizing began in India after independence, with then Prime Minister Nehru's *Discovery of India* and his effort to tell the history of India from an Indian perspective. Subsequently, several Indian academics, like K. R. Srinivasa Iyengar, C.D. Narasimhaiah, and others, including myself in my work, *Family Quarrels: Towards a Criticism of Indian Writing in English*, began the work of trying to create a criticism for Indian literature in English, free from European standards and European critics' perspectives. If we are going to decolonize, this should be our praxis. The received notion of postcolonial studies is that it was born in the wealthy ivory towers of Columbia, Harvard, and Essex; the latter is from where Homi Bhabha came. But this is not so. Literary critics from India, the African countries of Kenya, Nigeria, etc., were already decolonizing by creating new academic approaches written in English by Indian and African authors. Some found an identity of their own, under the umbrella of Commonwealth Literatures in English. But separate from this organization were C.D. Narasimhaiah's *Dhvanyaloka* and the Indian Institute of Advanced Studies. Scholars like Narasimhaiah articulated a criticism that would adequately represent and investigate how Indian literature and African literature written in English were to be measured.

In 1985, Frederic Jameson held at Duke a conference entitled "Third-World Literature in an Era of Multi National Capitalism," which became the basis of his much-cited article, published in 1986. Several significant authors and critics were invited to that conference, including Edward Said, Ngugi wa Thiong'o, Henry Louis Gates, and Homi Bhabha. It was at that conference that I met Ngugi and interviewed him along with Dennis Brutus. I mention this to point out that Ngugi wa Thiong'o was also at the forefront of the movement for decolonizing literatures and consciousnesses, long before the advent of postcolonial criticism. According to the book's frontispiece, parts of his influential book were delivered as lectures in 1981 at the Writer's Association of Kenya. At the same time, Chinwiezu's influential book *Decolonizing African Literature* was published in 1980. So, the sentiment for decolonizing literature and culture was in effect long before postcolonial theory came about. It was for the idea to decolonize that independence happened and a period post, i.e., after colonialism began. To use an adage, we cannot put the cart before the horse. And it is here that decolonial myth is essential when we can teach, narrate, keep alive the myths of our cultures, and or interpret the myths of our cultures to make them relevant to the issues of our times so that they emphasize for future generations the possibilities of seeing themselves in contradistinctions with the cultures that surround them; that these myths become both simultaneously decolonial and decolonizing. This practice has become urgent and essential in the current decolonial moment in the United States of America. Its pressing need to decolonize its past is contrarily a culture built on colonialism. It is this dichotomy that I want to capture in my knitting together the iconic women of the myths of three different cultures and of seeing them through the lens of the histories of the partitions of peoples and nation-building. It is essential to present the four myths of women characters that arise out of the waters, voice their cries together, and see them side by side to see how different moments of decoloniality are constructed. Hopefully, in the following discussions, I have thoroughly fleshed out each myth to see the parallels and why they are essential.

What do we understand by myths? They are placeholders of the culture, the receptacles that communicate the essence of the culture and pass it down. Hence, they are endemic to a culture and not open to colonization or alteration by any other culture's overlay. Myths were/are primarily oral tales, told by adults, patriarchs or matriarchs to children and communities, often didactic, but also in some ways anti-hegemonic. In the attempt to be didactic and to show the fall of a great man, the teller repeatedly criticized a king, a queen, or any power above the teller. Whether it was a Greek myth, an Indian or Persian myth, a tragedy or a comedy, a myth criticized a colonial administration or regime. It often functioned to bring down an individual, a power, or an empire. From Homer to the Mahabharata, myths chronicled battles, lives of great men, epic heroes, and their tragic encounters. They told of heroes or heroines overcoming conflicts with the mediation of "Gods, Daemons and Others," as R. K Narayan would've called them (75).

However, I believe that unless we move beyond politicized formulations of postcolonialism, and move beyond western critics' notions of postcolonialism, as propagated by South Asian theorists, myths and their decolonial import will never be decolonized. Even some prominent Postcolonial critics, Bhabha, Spivak, etc., especially those from the subcontinent, rely heavily on European theorists and their influences. Our notions of how literature can decolonize will never be fully decolonized unless we search for other relevant ways of reading. But since we cannot exist or function in a vacuum, we need to search for our theoretical bases from our local contact zones, as it were. In this effort, I have often turned to our theories of *rasa* and *dhvani*. However, I have turned to Joseph Campbell and his now widely accepted explications of myths and archetypes in this instance. I realize that Joseph Campbell is forever associated with George Lucas and *Star Wars* and thereby rejected by some academicians. For me, Joseph Campbell's in-depth study of Indian art and civilization in his book qualifies him to be a decolonial mythologist, one who studied the moments of contact of stories of the great civilizations in their contexts. His interpretations of the interconnectedness of heroes and heroines of several cultures keep him rooted and connected to the moments in history and society that render these myths relevant to us today. Campbell steeped himself into the world's cultures, almost becoming indigenous himself, as seen from his interviews with Bill Moyers. Campbell's *Correspondence: 1927-1977* (2019) shows extensive conversations with the Indian critic, philosopher, and culture explicator, Ananda Coomaraswamy, who wrote the now accepted interpretations of Indian culture in *The Dance of Shiva* (1924). This, I believe, legitimizes the use of Joseph Campbell for speaking about indigenous cultures. He is not looking at them as distant others, lumping them all together under a European perspective, which, interestingly, even Derrida and Algerian Jew do when looking at the other.

Joseph Campbell tells us that, "Myths are stories about the wisdom of life" (11). What does this wisdom incorporate? More often than not, myths are stories about the strength of the individual in the face of adversity. Where does the trouble come from? Frederic Jameson, in *The Political Unconscious* (1981), tells us:

> Evil thus, as Nietzsche taught us, continues to characterize whatever is radically different from me, whatever by virtue of precisely that difference seems to constitute a real and urgent threat to my own existence. So from the earliest times, the stranger from another tribe, the barbarian, who speaks an incomprehensible language and follows outlandish customs, but also the woman, whose biological difference stimulates fantasies of castration and devoration, or in our own time, the avenger of accumulated resentments from some oppressed class or race, or else that alien being Jew or Communist, behind whose apparently human features a malignant and preternatural intelligence is thought to lurk: these are some of the archetypal figures of the Other, about whom the essential point to be made is not so much that he is feared because; rather he is evil because he is 'Other,' alien, different strange unclean and unfamiliar. (115)

And so, it is that daemons are depicted with horrific features, preternaturally ugly colored in differing colors from ancient texts through magazines, comics, movies, from Bollywood films to Telugu films to American films like *Avatar* to emphasize the other and otherness, thus repeating, emphasizing and imprinting upon the mind of readers, particularly children, fear of the other.

But is that the purpose of myth? As often presented to us, the purpose of myth is to glorify the hero or heroine: the call to adventure, the meeting with the goddess, the magical flight, the apostasies, or apotheosis. But what is a Decolonial myth? Is it a myth that turns the traditional myth upside down? Or is it a decolonizing myth, a myth that tells a tale with a subtext urging decolonization? Decolonial, or decolonial praxis, as we know, is an exceptional term often promulgated through the work of Walter Mignolo and Catherine Walsh. "Decoloniality," Mignolo and Walsh tell us, is different from "decolonization" (37). Decoloniality recognizes the moment of coloniality and is the unveiling of coloniality instead of a simple resistance against colonialism. In their introduction to *On Decoloniality*, Mignolo and Walsh wrote:

> A return of right-wing nationalists in the West (i.e., European Union plus Britain and the United States) is not worse, from a decolonial perspective than the continuation of neoliberal globalism. However, the new world ordering of coloniality forces us to ask: what do decoloniality and decolonization mean in this junction? The reasons should be obvious: decolonization during the Cold War meant the struggle for the liberation of the third world and, when successful, the formation of nation-states claiming sovereignty. By the 1990s, decolonization's failure in most nations had become clear; with the state in the hands of minority elites, the patterns of colonial power continued both internally (i.e., internal colonialism) and the relation to global structures. At that moment, coloniality was unveiled. Decoloniality was born in the unveiling of decoloniality. (6)

The Myth of La Llorona: An Example

Emma Perez, in her book *The Decolonial Imaginary: Writing Chicanas into History* (1999), tells us that her category "the decolonial imaginary" was born from a consideration of the myth of La Llorona (84). Spanish chroniclers of the conquest heroized her for standing by Cortéz. But Mexican nationalists considered her a Malinche or traitor, even *La Chingada* (an abusive term). Perez writes, "This new category, the decolonial imaginary, can help us rethink history in a way that makes Chicana/o agency transformative" (5). For me, it is a clear example of how ancient stories create new spaces. And it is from the new space of understanding that decolonization follows.

In this writing, in June of 2020, the central myth of the Southwestern United States' Hispanic corridor is that of La Llorona. It has taken on a pressing urgency because it tells the story of Hispanic colonization when Black Lives Matter calls into question all symbols and monuments of colonial histories. It tells the story of the first Hispanic colonizers to land on American soil long before the Jamestown settlers. And yet, the other myths I develop later are equally essential to be retained here in this essay for comparison because they shed light on this myth and how myths shape contemporary thinking when they enlighten the point of contact between the oppressor and the oppressed. They also reinforce the archetype of the strong woman who emerges after dissolution, as it were. La Llorona has become central to the struggle of

Hispanic migration into the US and the current race crisis and objections to all who held slaves, including the Spanish conquistadors who owned indigenous slaves. Llorona, or Malinché as she is called, her real name is unknown and clouded by names she was called, was Native Mexican or Aztec. Hernan Cortéz was a white Spaniard. The children she kills and buries are mixed-race or mestizo, and hence, her myth becomes one of the preservations of the race or *raza*. She disowns her mixed-race children. This call for *raza* is later picked up by the Chicanos in their call for Chicano power. Hispanic migration into the USA is a double-edged sword. Hispanics are both the colonized (by the contemporary majority) and the colonialists because, from the 1500s, they colonized the entire central corridor of the North American continent from Mexico City to Colorado.

This is also important in the Black Lives Matter movement's urgency to remove statues seen as symbols of oppression. Though the myth of La Llorona (character) focuses on the first Hispanic colonizer, Hernan Cortéz, he is soon followed by Juan de Oñate, a particularly ruthless *conquistador*, who is said to have cut off the feet of the Acoma people and tossed them down from the Mesa or table-top plateau that stands as a butte over the passageway into Albuquerque. Protesters fought to remove the statue, much to the chagrin of those Hispanics who both see themselves as having lost a part of their heritage and as an oppressed minority. From the protesters' point of view, they are protesting all matters seen as oppressive, even this population, which is often considered an oppressed discriminated against minority ethnic group. Hispanics then are, in fact, also regarded as perpetrators of colonialism. Nowhere but in this current situation, the Hispanic's precarious position in the USA has been more poignantly showcased. The statue depicted the moment of contact of the colonizer: Onate, with a stagecoach and a following of peoples, including Indian slaves. Tearing down the statue is turned into a moment for decolonization. Yet, it depends upon the decolonized and oppresses a minority by further marginalizing them by portraying them as colonialists. It is an immense irony and a paradox.

Let us examine the myth, originally an oral tale, a piece of urban folklore, often used to scare children into bedtime, is now written as a novella and produced as a movie. The movie came at the moment of hostility towards the new Hispanic migration into America, i.e., when the Central American refugees sought asylum. The Trump administration blocked oppressed migrants who were walking into the border from the central Americas. It was seen as a scare tactic that doubled back on the original meaning of the legend. Parents told children that Llorona would come to get them if they didn't go to bed by a particular hour. They were also telling them that *La Migra*, or immigration, was coming for them. On the other hand, as widely publicized in the media, the

Trump administration told the American people that if they did not stem the migrant tides, the migrants would come and get them, their jobs, their homes, their sustenance, etc.

The Legend of La Llorona is the story of a mother who kills her children to preserve her *raza* (race), identity, sense of self, pride at being Indio/Aztec, native Mexican, unadulterated by the Hispanics into whom she intermarries. She is the mother of the mestizos. But she wants to put an end to that line when the man betrays her; she thought he was loyal to her. She is at once the betrayer and the betrayed, dealing with the feared 'Other' who, in this case, is the Hispanic colonizer, colonizing Mexico in the name of Isabella of Spain. So, identity and the question of the purity of race are underlined in this myth, and it is still so in Northern New Mexico. Llorona is Malinché or a traitor, a traitor for having married a white man and children. To be of mixed race is to be *mestizo* is *pocho*.

In the USA Southwest, where I have lived and taught for forty years, first at the University of Texas at El Paso, and now at the University of New Mexico in Albuquerque, *raza* embodies racial purity, cultural pride, and resistance. It is *orgullo*, or pride in culture and satisfaction in the way of being. Politicized theorists believe that it is a word only associated with the Chicano movement and embodied in the politics of Chicanismo/a, or Cesár Chavez. I live at the intersection of Avenida César Chávez and Route 66, in an at once interestingly colonial and decolonial space that embodies stories of settlements. And it represents the mingling of peoples and their stories. Hispanos do not necessarily identify themselves as Chicano express *raza*, or pride in their race.

On the other hand, most people of Spanish heritage in the USA don't want to see themselves as Chicano because of the baggage of politics. In Northern New Mexico, Hispanos prefer to be Spanish. This has been very visibly shaken up in the recent activities around the Black Lives Matter movement. In my new hometown of Albuquerque recently, this sense of race and pride was heightened when in the fury of activity to demolish statues associated with colonialism, activists wanted to tear down the statue of Juan de Oñate. But Northern New Mexicans wanted it to be preserved as an emblem of their settlement. Many New Mexicans who see themselves mainly as white Hispanics and have an immense sense of pride in their relation to the land of New Mexico did not want to see this happen. But they are also a minority, albeit a colonizing culture. How were they to be accommodated in this frenzy? Yes, Juan de Oñate was a ruthless colonizer. As he came up this corridor towards what is now Colorado, confronted by the Acoma Indians, in sheer self-defense and survival and fear of scalping, he threw them off the plateau after cutting off their feet so that they could not run after the invading hordes of Spaniards. To him, it was probably self-defense of himself and his party. It is granted that the land is originally Native American, but in the palimpsest of colonialisms, the Spanish or Hispanic/Latino who came first was then colonized by the white Americans. So, the history of Hispanics and their pride in their belonging to the USA Southwest is an issue of double jeopardy. It is further complicated by the intermingling of races, the Spanish and the Native Americans producing the *mestizo* who is often counted as Chicano or chico, little Mexicano, a counting not welcomed by the Northern New Mexicans. The only Albuquerque City councillor to object to the tearing down of the statue was a woman who saw herself as directly descendent from the pure Spanish, an attitude similar to being Daughters of the American Revolution (DAR). In and through the Black Lives movement and the search for solidarities all these senses of race begin to dilute. Who is to have solidarity with whom, mainly when there are resentments and competitiveness of jobs and quotas between the two ethnic minorities? This is true of *Dalit* and Muslim interactions in India. Who are the oppressed and the oppressor?

In the novel *The Legend of La Llorona* (1984), Rudolfo Anaya wrote that the myth of the purple snake god of the Aztecs saw in the mirror and thought, "I am dark, I could not possibly be god" (54). So, he told his people that he would return when he was "white" (56). He also added:

> it was not only the end of an era that preoccupied the Aztecs in that fateful year of 1516; there was something more ominous in the air. At the root of the Aztec soul there was a legend whose prophecy filled the people with doubts and fears. According to the legend, this was the year the god Quetzalcoatl was destined to return from his exile in the East. (10)

The people, who awaited the god, saw white sailing ships and sails coming over the waters. Believing that it was, in fact, their god who had returned now that he was white, they fell and worshipped the white people embarking from the ships. Anaya does not name the colonizer, calling him only the Captain. One indigenous woman takes it upon herself to help him make his way through the strange land Cortéz sees as paradise. The indigene befriends him, even learning the Spanish language and teaching him the Nahuatl language so she can speak with his people, and helps him make his way, not realizing that it was a colonial endeavor. Malinche, or traitor as she is called now (her name becoming synonymous with traitorship), later on, enters into a relationship with Cortéz and bears him three children. It is not until Isabella of Spain comes to inspect her colonies, on behalf of Don Carlos, the king, that Malinche realizes that Cortéz is betrothed to Isabella and means to abandon Malinche and take her sons back him to Spain. At that point, Malinche consults a priest, who tells her that she must take an obsidian knife, stab her children and drown them in the waters around the lake of Tenochtitlan to save the race and Mexico itself. She arises out of the water as a crying woman and La Llorona (character).

She is now along the US Mexican border and in the myths and legends along the southwestern border, a living legend or myth, a bogeywoman by whom children are scared and told that Llorona is coming to get them. These days this myth has become a poignantly fear-inducing reality in the lives of children who are separated from their parents by Immigration and Customs Enforcement (ICE). Today, the myth of La Llorona also features in a horror film. Still, more importantly, it is a myth of the border crises, the separation of children, and the ever-present immigration officer. More than twenty years ago, the Chicana author Sandra Cisneros wrote about the women crossing the border in her epic novel/collection of stories *Woman Hollering Creek* (1991).

Coloniality is unveiled when Malinche realizes that Cortéz has been a colonizer, and he has used Malinche and betrayed her and her people. But, she has been unable to speak, and her only act of resistance is to kill her children: "the most hideous crime of womanhood, the unforgiveable crime of a mother, the unspoken terror" (Anaya 88). "Malinche," the Captain whispered her name softly. "Our wrongs have led you to this terrible deed. Our wrongs are beyond all human understanding." "Yes, I have been wronged," Malinche answered, standing tall and noble before them. "My sons were to be made slaves, and I paid for their liberation dearly. Now they are dead but other sons of Mexico will rise against you and avenge this deed. The future will not forgive any of us. I, Malinche princess and mother of the Mexicans, will forever be known as the woman who cries for her sons" (Anaya 10). The silently suffering Malinche has finally spoken. In Postcolonial theory, of course, we ask the repeated question, as articulated by Gayatri Spivak in her essay "Can the Subaltern Speak?" But, when the speaking voice of the subaltern, the subjugated one, is taken, there is always death, murder, and mayhem. The murder and mayhem that Spivak is referring to is the Indian practice of *sati*, which, as Spivak articulates it, is an act of freedom. Spivak repeatedly says that she isn't advocating widow burning, or *Jauhar*, mass suicide to save one's honor, but sees both as acts of freedom and self-will on the part of the women. And this is how it is articulated in Anaya's *The Legend of La Llorona*, an all-pervasive myth of the US's southern border. Malinche's suicide is a form of *jauhar* suicide, in the face of colonial oppression, a form of resistance to save one's face and race. Thus, the subaltern speaks in the fearful cry of the howling wind, the voice that emerges from the dark waters.

Now Spivak's argument regarding the subaltern is, of course, problematic. Is she advocating that women be allowed to practice *sati* or the more extended *jauhar* as she seems to be doing? In "Can the Subaltern Speak?" Spivak absolves herself by writing, "Obviously I am not advocating the killing of widows. I am suggesting that within the two contending versions of freedom, the constitution of the female subject in life is the place of the differend" (92). She does not want superstition or the ritual to be defined as a crime. In this context, we can see Malinche's act as one asserting freedom for her children and all children of Mexico.

The whole controversy over the recent Indian film of *Padmavati*, which resurrected the debate over *Jauhar* or mass suicide, both heroizing and denigrating it, can be seen as an act of freedom. The film portrayed the effort of the Hindu women and princesses to save each other from rape by the invading colonizing force, which in this case happened to be the Muslim conquerors, just like the Spanish colonizers in the case of *La Llorona* (the movie). Spivak problematizes this concept/custom: "Although *jauhar* is not, strictly speaking, an act of *sati*, and although I do not wish to speak for the sanctioned sexual violence of conquering male armies, Moslem or otherwise, female self-immolation in the face of it is a legitimation of rape as natural, and works in the long run in the interest of unique genital possession of the female" (99). So, she sees *jauhar* more as an act of surrender, giving power to the males. In mythological terms, though, it is heroized as an act of resistance against the colonizing oppressor. But it does not allow the woman/women to speak out or to create a decolonizing movement. She does this by resisting surrendering her beloved children and raising her voice, even if it is in screams, rising out of the waters. Women's voices were growing out of waters as they were drowning or becoming more symbolic in later European literary myths.

There is a similar myth of collective suicide in Parsi lore, where the Parsi women, who were in fact immigrants, to India from Persia, due to the Muslim persecution and were diasporic seekers of shelter in a Hindu kingdom, committed mass suicide when the host culture of the Hindus, terrorized them in the wake of their inability to pay a crushing tax. Karl Kerawala, in a Facebook post on Universal Zoroastrianism Art and Culture, tells of an incident around the 11th century, when Parsis had settled in a village called Variav in Gujarat near the river Tapi. But when they became highly prosperous, the hosting Rajah demanded a tax and sent armies to collect it. While the men were off fighting and the Muslims threatened the women, they put on the men's armor and fought the troops. However, the Hindu armies soon realized that they were fighting women when they saw their faces. Ashamed, they doubled their efforts to defeat the women who, in their weariness, rushed into the river and drowned themselves. For the women, it was an act of saving themselves from being possessed or colonized. It is a myth that today legitimizes the prevention of intermarriage, both with Muslims, who were the cause of the uprooting of the Hindus. The women spoke with their actions but weren't allowed to talk face to face to argue for their rights.

The most effective trope for decoloniality and decolonizing in this chapter lies in my reading of Hans Christian Anderson's *The Little Mermaid* (1837). I use the story of the Little Mermaid as told by Anderson and as depicted by Disney (though the Disney version corrupts the ending and turns the postcolonial message into one of hybridity) routinely to teach postcolonialism.

Let us look at the story. A white colonizing European prince comes aboard a ship to the Caribbean. Due to a Tempest, he is shipwrecked on an island. A curious mermaid makes her way into the ship, and as she sees the beautiful, blonde Prince on the beach, she instantly falls in love with him. Everything is different. This is her first encounter with the other, and otherness is everywhere. In the Disney film, the mermaid discovers "the forks, knives, and statues that make up the ship's cargo" (Anderson 78). But what the Prince hears is the gentle, sweet singing of the mermaid, which wakes him in his unfamiliar surroundings. Like the Spanish colonizer in *La Llorona*, the Prince seeks the woman who can be his guide. But, in her otherness, she is ashamed to be seen, recognized, and named. So, she goes to the Sea Witch in the film, *Ursula*, to become a recognizable Subject.

Spivak, drawing on Derrida writes, about "the *European* Subject's tendency to constitute the other as marginal" (89). And so, the mermaid attempts to give up who she is and her identity to become what would be acceptable to the European. Fanon reminds of this in his *Black Skin, White Masks* as the colonized other attempts to become like the colonizer for the sake of acceptance. In the "Foreword: Remembering Fanon" to *Black Skin, White Masks*, Homi Bhabha writes that, "to exist is to be called into being in relation to an Otherness," or again, "It is precisely in that ambivalent use of different — to be different from those that are different makes you the same" (xi). She trades her fins for legs which Anderson tells us to feel like swords stabbing into her. But the actual test comes when she has to give up her voice to the devious Sea witch, whose intention is to capture the Prince. That is the ultimate indigene's sacrifice: giving up the ability to speak out and become one with the superior other. Of course, when she gives up her ability to speak, she gives up her identity, her ability to be recognized as the one who saved the man by her singing which awakened him, the man she loves and wants to be identified.

This is the ultimate colonial mentality of the individual who has internalized the colonizer, who then sacrifices herself for the colonizer. In the original Anderson story, her sacrifice is that she commits suicide and becomes seafoam on the water as she watches the deceptive Sea-witch take over her love. In attempting to make it contemporary, Disney Studios makes the wrong right and allows the mermaid to expose the Sea witch and be recognized by the Prince for a happy ending, a happy ending of hybridity. But we know the truth that in a world dogged by new nationalism, hybridity is not acceptable. We are consistently recognized as the other. In this, the little mermaid is the subaltern who can't speak, as opposed to La Llorona, who, at least in the Anaya version, speaks out by screaming forcefully. In the mythic legend, all she does is cry out. But it is in the crying out that she is reminding children and Hispanic peoples in general of their colonization and colonial heritage. Llorona arises out of the water, and this story is told repeatedly to remind one of the decolonizing efforts in which we should be involved.

Myths of Women and Water

Myths and images of women arising out of the water constitute a coming to an awareness of one's nationalism, of one's connection to the landscape, the land. The woman arising out of the water, I believe, is central in both decolonial and decolonizing myth, decolonial because it enacts the moment of the recognition of coloniality, and from it flows the decolonizing effort the return to indigenous roots, exactly what Spivak would reject as the nostalgia for lost origins.

We all know that James Joyce's *Portrait of the Artist as a Young Man* is a bildungsroman or the story of a young man. In traditional bildungsroman, this awareness is simply the awakening of adulthood, of being embodied and engendered. More recently, we look at the bildungsroman as a manifestation of one's sense of identity, coming into an awareness of belonging. In *Portrait of the Artist as a Young Man*, the two come together as Stephen feels his first flush of sexuality in seeing the image of a bird-woman coming out of the water, an idea that excites him, but from which he turns away. Is she Leda? Is she an Irish *Tuata da dannan*, the pre-Christian Irish race? Or is she some female manifestation of the family of Cucuhlain? As Joyce says in the *Portrait of the Artist as a Young Man*:

> A girl stood before him in midstream, alone and still, gazing out to sea. She seemed like one whom Magic had changed into the likeness of a strange and beautiful sea bird. Her long slender bare legs were delicate as a crane's and pure save where an emerald trail of seaweed had fashioned itself a sign upon the flesh. Her thighs, fuller and soft-hued as ivory, were bared almost to the hips where the white fringes of her drawers were like featherings of soft white down. Her slate-blue skirts were kilted boldly about her waist and dovetailed behind her. Her bosom was as a bird's, soft and slight. Her image had passed into his soul forever, and no word had broken the holy silence of his ecstasy. (220)

She is, in fact, Yeats' Leda, Yeats' Irish monomyth, a connection to Ireland, Irishness, and Irish Nationalism. But Stephen turns away. Or does he?

In D.H. Lawrence's novel *The Plumed Serpent*, Lawrence, living in the US Southwest, in Taos, New Mexico, travels to Mexico and attempts to create a new religion, a mixture of the Anglo Saxon and the Azatlan. In his novel, he imagines his patroness from Taos, Mabel Dodge Luhan, as Kate, an elite English visitor. She is visiting a politician called Don Ramon in Mexico.

This is Kate, who had said that she could never be an authentic Mexican. She had described a bullfight as abominable, Mexico as uncivilized, primitive, and primal, and its efforts towards democracy a failure because of the vast class differences and Mexican politicians. But Kate, having been married to an Irish freedom fighter, had roots in other independence movements. So, she does allow herself to be identified with the cause of liberating Mexico from the Spaniards and the Catholic Church. "Mexico is another Ireland," she says (Lawrence 14). She goes from Mexico, meaning to her only "the mass of silent peons pelados, Indians," mere natives, to wanting only the comfort of Don Ramon and "the Hymns of Quetzalcoatl" (Lawrence 18). "There is a bit of horror in it, and I don't want horror in my soul," and yet, like Kurtz, she has embraced the horrors (Lawrence 21).

She has a beautiful, romantic ceremonial marriage with Cipriano and then suddenly comes to her identity as English. "I am Kate Forrester–loathsome really to be called Malintzi!" (Lawrence 23). By contrasting herself with the myth, she comes into an awareness of her national identity. So, myths play a crucial role in one's coming into one's understanding of self. Kate witnesses the gruesome ceremonial murders–almost like Malinche's killing of her children and drowning them as in the myth of the La Llorona. In this, the formal act, literal and metaphoric of the killing of the children of the Colonizers–these children are the sacrificial lambs just like in Ireland/Tuatha de Danaan. She emerges from this a *criada* (a crying woman) *la Gritona* and La Llorona, who longs for England but finds her place by Don Cipriano like Mable found and lived out her days with Tony, the indigene of Taos.

Conclusion

In his extensive writings, Joseph Campbell has shown us that myth is essential to self-awareness. In the nationalist bildungsroman or in the myths of coming into a national awareness, the mythic structure of the hero's journey and the apotheosis is the decolonizing that results from the decolonial moment, i.e., through the coming into an awareness of belonging in their ordinary world, through an encounter with the colonizer or other. We can see this in stories as vastly different as the nationalist myth of *La Llorona*, or Joyce's account of Ireland as told in *Portrait*, or even a simple children's story like that of the *Little Mermaid*. Classical myth and classical mythic structure are crucial to the creation of the myth of a nation. Thus, all myth is essentially a decolonial moment.

Works Cited

Ahmed, A. *Colonial discourse and Postcolonial Theory.* Columbia University Press, 1992. Print.

Anaya, Rudolfo A. *The Legend of La Llorona.* Tonatiuh-Quinto Sol, 1984. Print.

Anderson, Hans Christian. *The Little Mermaid.* C.A. Reitzel, 1837. Print.

Bhabha, Homi. Foreword: Remembering Fanon. *Black Skin, White Masks.* By Frantz Fanon. Pluto Press, 1986. vii-xxvi. Print.

Campbell, Joseph. *Correspondence: 1927–1987.* Harvard University Press, 2019. Print.

Cisneros, Sandra. *Woman Hollering Creek and Other Stories.* Random House, 1991. Print.

Jameson, Fredric. *The Political Unconscious.* Cornell University Press, 1981. Print.

Joyce, James. *A Portrait of the Artist as a Young Man.* Penguin, 1992. Print.

Lawrence, D. H. *The Plumed Serpent.* Cambridge University Press, 2002. Print.

Marx, Karl. "British Rule in India." *Marxist.org,* 16 Mar. 2021, www.marxist.org/archive/marx/works/1853/06/25.htm.

Mignolo, Walter, and Catherine E. Walsh. *On Decoloniality: Concepts, Analytics, Praxis.* Duke University Press, 2018. Print.

Narayan, R.K. *Gods, Daemons and Others.* University Press of Chicago, 1964. Print.

Perez, Emma. *The Decolonial Imaginary: Writing Chicanas into History.* Indiana University Press, 1999. Print.

Said, E.W. *Orientalism.* Pantheon Books, 1978. Print.

Spivak, Gayatri Chakravorty. "Can the Subaltern Speak?" *Colonial Discourse and Post-Colonial Theory.* Ed. Patrick Williams and Laura Chrisman. Columbia University Press, 1994. 66-111. Print.

Part II
Decoloniality:
Experiences and Engagements

Chapter 5

White as Paper, Black as Ink: Bilali Muhammad and the Transdisciplinary Imperative

Adam Short
Soccer Coach, Richmond, Virginia

Abstract

One of the great challenges in decoloniality is the sheer scope of the apparatus that creates, sustains, and enforces a colonial perspective. All the many layers of colonial culture co-construct the picture of reality favored by the colonizer, and this system of bias in inclusion / or exclusion of certain stories in the canon persists long after the original structures of repression have disappeared, mutated, or evolved. To correct this bias, decoloniality must engage intentionally and at a level of specificity sufficiently to allow the identification of the actual mechanisms of inclusion and exclusion that systematically favor certain stories over others. This chapter looks at one specific story – the epic tale of Bilali Muhammad – and identifies the tropes the story violates that prevent it from being told, even during a time when Hollywood is hungry for scripts incorporating themes of black liberation. Further, it shows how the distinct Muslim character of the Bilali Muhammad story makes it especially dissonant with the fictionalized version of black history usually presented by Hollywood.

Keywords: decoloniality, colonial culture, specificity, Bilali Muhammad, black liberation, fictionalized version.

* * *

Introduction

In his 2014 book *The Walking Qu'ran*, Rudolph Ware shows that "classical Qu'ran schooling and its contemporary manifestations in West Africa are based on what were once broadly held Islamic ideals about educating the whole of the human being rather than the narrow transmission of discursive knowledge" (54). Furthermore, Ware traces the story of how West African Muslims have, since at least 1770, focused on the human body itself as a crucial tool "to archive, transmit, decode and actualize religious knowledge" (3-4).

To a scholar of West African Islamic history in the Americas, it might seem surprising that Bilali Muhammad's name does not come up in Ware's book. After all, Bilali's biography, a story that is among the best-known of all the many millions of stories of enslaved Africans in the Americas before the US Civil War, is that of a man who came across the Atlantic with nothing but his body and was able to transmit a living Islamic culture that endured in coastal Georgia and the Geechee/Gullah diaspora for many generations.

A look at the history of Bilali's story and its relationship to the formal record suggests a possible explanation. Given the amount of confusion in the traditional literature about Bilali and his project, it is plausible that even in an interdisciplinary study such as Ware's, it would be challenging to recognize Bilali's importance to the thesis by relying on scholarly sources alone, even though Bilali stepped off a slave ship in Middle Caicos sometimes shortly after 1770 with nothing but his body and his ability to write Arabic, a literal walking Qu'ran.

Fortunately, Bilali's story is already in its ascendancy informal literature. al-Ahari has shown using *Tashif*, the Islamic science of studying texts with diacritical marks, to understand how the author of the text spoke that Bilali's manuscript is not a reproduction but an original work of Muslim jurisprudence. While the document does follow the structure of the *Risalah* of Ibn Abi Zayd al-Qayrawani of Tunisia, it contains original ideas not present in the *Risalah*, such as, "belief enters the heart more strongly through practice" (al-Ahari 5).

Fortunately, the modern scholar has many sources at her disposal besides the formal record. For this reason, the story of Bilali, his manuscript, and the bequest he left behind offer useful evidence of the necessity of a transdisciplinary approach to decolonial scholarship so that the various threads of knowledge possessed by different strands of culture can be brought together to create a clearer picture of the link between West African Islam and her diaspora in the Americas.

Bilali and his *Meditations*

Bilali Muhammad was a Muslim jurisprudent, agricultural scientist, military leader, and founding father of the American republic. He died under conditions of enslavement on a plantation in the Georgia Sea Islands in 1859. Unlike most enslaved people, Bilali's story is comparatively well-known today for two interconnected reasons. First, he left behind a long manuscript, called "The Diary of Ben Ali" but recently more accurately referred to either as *The Bilali*

Document or *Meditations* (name of the work) detailing the practice of Islam as it was understood by the inhabitants of Sapelo Island "in the early part of the 19th century" (al-Ahari 11). Second, a network of people that includes Bilali, his descendants, and others has consistently worked to keep Bilali's name and teachings alive in oral and written traditions of the Geechee/Gullah diaspora from his death until the present day.

Dabovic notes that the Muslim slave narratives are distinctive. They comprise not only remembrances of the past and commentaries on the present horrors of slavery but also a future-focused project "to address a future generation of Muslims and establish the boundaries of the *umma* or Islamic community" (111). Unique to such a task under conditions of slavery and oppression is the quality of *opacity* – creating understandable documents primarily to those who are meant to read and understand them and incomprehensible to others. Such techniques are standard in Muslim teachers who operate in conditions of necessary secrecy, as related by Idries Shah.

As to the contents of the document itself, given its extraordinary cultural and historical significance as the first surviving work of Islamic jurisprudence ever produced in west of the Atlantic Ocean, Bilali's *Meditations* is a surprisingly little work. It is thirteen pages long and comprises a few pages of devotion to Allah, a promise of protection and reward for believers, some lines of prayer, and a description of how to practice ablution (the ritual washing of the body). It is a manual for the proper practice of Islam and a little more. However, with its discussion of the path (*sirat*) and gnostic devotion (*dhikr*), the sixth page provides a potentially interesting jumping-off point for investigating Bilali's possible connection to some Sufi order.

Though Dabovic provides a slightly different account of the confusion than does Austin, both scholars agree that at least until 1939, no one had owned the *Meditations* since Francis Goulding's death in 1881 or had any idea at all what the document said, or even what it was. It is possible that Francis Goulding was ignorant on this matter as well. In general, there seemed to be a conviction, primarily evident in an affidavit given to the University of Georgia in 1930 by Goulding's son, an unreconstructed Southerner, according to Austin, that was the personal diary of a white Arab overseer named Ben Ali.

It may strain credulity for the modern reader to encounter the idea that there was confusion about whether Bilali Muhammad – the name means Black Muhammad and he was routinely described as "coal-black" (Austin 268) – was, in fact, a black man. However, as Ian Haney López shows in *White by Law*, white and black are not a simple matter because the boundaries of these distinctions are constantly changing. Judgments in individual cases are influenced by myriad factors grounded in the legal structures that define racial boundaries in a particular society.

White as Paper, Black as Ink: The Myth of Ben Ali

By 1930, when Charles Goulding presented the Bilali Document to the University of Georgia, whether a person is white had primarily superseded whether a person is black. This happened because of a series of court cases concerning the eligibility of various applicants for US citizenship. Under federal law until 1952, only a white person was eligible to be naturalized as a US citizen, but the statute, in place since 1790, did not define what it meant to be white. Thus, it fell to the courts to judge the legal whiteness of each individual who applied to immigrate to the United States, as at that time, only persons eligible for naturalization were allowed to immigrate.

The doctrine applied in these cases was called the common-sense doctrine, an overt repudiation of any scientific or other objective bases for defining racial categories. The courts found that objective criteria seemed too often to lead to the wrong answers about who was white, and therefore, it was best to simply allow judges to use their subjective judgment to decide whether someone ought to be considered white or not.

The existence of this *ad hoc* racial system in the early 19th-century sheds some light on how the myth of Ben Ali could have begun in Charles Goulding's mind. In this period, standard criteria used by the courts in declaring a person white included the ability to read and write, speak English, advanced artisanal skills, knowledge of agricultural techniques, and other markers of being "civilized" (López 20). Since Bilali possessed all of these qualities, it may have seemed self-evident to Goulding that Bilali must have been white by law despite being African-born.

A close reading of contemporary accounts of Bilali makes clear that during Bilali's lifetime, there was ample confusion, not about Bilali's whiteness (given his enslavement that possibility was perhaps too uncomfortable to contemplate) but about his blackness. This confusion was possible but necessary to preserve the favored propaganda framework of Southern whites in the 19th century.

One of the central challenges I encountered in studying Bilali is that the space his story occupies in history is such that accounts of his life, no matter where they appear, are almost always offered as part of some overtly political project that necessarily includes prevailing attitudes about race, of which Bilali is often a salient example. Thus, information gleaned about Bilali from the historical record can rarely, if ever, be taken at face value.

Commander of the Faithful: Kingsley's Bilali in Wartime

The first mention of Bilali Muhammad in the surviving literature is an exciting and counterintuitive example. In his writings quoted by Austin and numerous others, Zephaniah Kingsley relates the British raids that harassed the Georgia Sea Islands during and after 1812. Kingsley writes that Thomas Spalding, owner of the Sapelo Island plantation where Bilali and his family were enslaved, entrusted Bilali with the island's defense by commanding a substantial force of eighty enslaved musketeers. According to Kingsley's account, Bilali accepted the command with a swashbuckling boast: "I will answer for every Negro of the true faith, but none of the *Christian dogs* that you own!" (cited in Kingsley 68).

This story is astonishing in its implications on several levels, but perhaps most important is what it highlights about the context Kingsley offers to the account. At the time, he was living in Florida. He was involved in an unknown type of political activism having to do with resistance to the imposition in coastal Florida of the US racial caste system, in which black people were a permanent underclass and the displacement of the multi-tiered Spanish system that had prevailed in Florida before it was ceded to the US in 1821. In the Spanish system, black slaves were still the bottom caste, but other "semi-black" (Fleszar 135) caste levels created some element of social mobility for enslaved people.

Kingsley published an anonymous treatise in 1828 (and again in 1829 under his name) arguing that slavery could and should be preserved as an American institution (indeed, he viewed slavery as a social imperative that could never be abolished entirely), but that the system needed to be administered in such a way that it is free of cruelty and that "amalgamates with the ordinary conditions of life" (Kingsley 148).

Kingsley is offering his account of Bilali's valor and Spalding's trust in him, explicitly as an example of a slave system working as he believes a slave system should, allowing a distinction between common African slaves and a more civilized, competent class of enslaved people who could be trusted with greater responsibility, including potentially the duties of freedom. However, it is essential to remember that Kingsley's vision is mainly theoretical, as Georgia and Florida are in practice engaged in passing laws to outlaw black freedom entirely.

Kingsley, a Quaker who practiced polygamy by marrying several emancipated women that he previously had enslaved and who carefully willed his plantation to his mixed-race family, was idiosyncratic in many ways. Still, some of his attitudes that might strike the modern reader as inexplicable or contradictory were fairly standard among Sea Island plantation owners or became so by 1840.

An underappreciated element of Southern antebellum culture is the prominence in the Southern discourse of what modern political philosopher Lorna Finlayson has called the "illusion of dissent" (64), wherein an essentially monolithic social attitude masquerades as a robust debate. In the Antebellum

South, many plantation owners by 1840 fancied themselves as abolitionists or at least styled themselves that way. This was the case with two particular plantation owners who mentioned Bilali in their public writings and their correspondence with one another, William Hodgson and James Couper.

Brothers in the Faith: Hodgson's Bilali as Fulani Exemplar

Hodgson is not an abolitionist in any sense of the word that might be accepted today. Still, one of the central themes of his *Notes on Northern Africa, the Sahara and Soudan* (1844) is his professed interest in "the future civilization of Africa, and the consequent suppression of the external slave trade" (52). In other words, Hodgson believes that by furthering the cause of European missionaries in Africa, he is working to stop the horrors of transatlantic slavery from which he is actively engaged in profiting. For Hodgson, the reason for the existence of slavery is the inherent inferiority of black African civilization. Thus, the only path to ending the African slave trade is European Christians' forceful imposition of culture on Africans. In Hodgson's view, this principle is axiomatic, so much so that it is impervious to being punctured even by clear contradictory evidence. Indeed, his chapter on the Fulani people begins with an assertion of the 19th-century race science, claiming that the Fulani are not black but classified adequately as somewhere between Arabs and black people.

Hodgson's exposure to the Fulani people – the dominant ethnic group in the portion of Africa Hodgson, is studying – has made it impossible for him to continue to classify them as non-civilized. Thus, to preserve his propaganda framework, he must find some way to organize the Fulani as non-black.

This technique – of delegitimizing black civilization as a first resort but denying the blackness of civilized people as a last resort – is endemic in the 19th century white justifications of slavery and anti-black racism. Its utility is obvious – it protects the racist propaganda framework from all possible counterevidence. Indeed, the technique is so transparent and ubiquitous that it might read as comical if its consequences to the fate of so many millions, both then and continuing to modern times, were not so dire.

Once Hodgson is satisfied that he has proved his initial assertion that "the Foulah are not Negroes" (54), he is free to move on to his genuine interest in the Fulani – as potential allies in the European project of ending the slave trade by imposing Christian civilization on Africans. Here, after all, are civilized African people living and working among the uncivilized African tribes, of whom the unwashed hordes are less likely to be wary.

This idea is self-refuting – if the dominant ethnic group in Northern Africa is a proper civilization, in what sense does Northern Africa need to be civilized by Europeans? – does not seem to have crossed Hodgson's mind. It is armed with an understanding of the mindset that produced such profound cognitive dissonance that I evaluate Hodgson's account of Bilali Muhammad's friend Salih Bilali, which he provides in the form of some correspondence that he has had with another Sea Island plantation owner, James Couper of St. Simon's Island.

This may have been troubling to Couper, as through his scholarship and his friendship with the more distinguished and learned Hodgson, he has come to understand that the Fulani are civilized and that enslaving them is therefore problematic. Fortunately for Couper's conscience, it turns out that most of the Fulani speakers on St. Simon's are not ethnic Fulani but familiar black people who have acquired the language by having been for some time in servitude among that nation. There is one fly in the ointment; however, a man Couper calls Tom. Tom is an ethnic Fulani originally from Mali by way of the British-controlled Bahamas who goes by the name Salih Bilali among the other enslaved Africans at St. Simon's.

This discovery that Tom is a Fulani seems to be a great relief to Couper, as he can unburden himself of a set of facts which before he had thought objectionable, or at least uncomfortable. Once again, in the case of Kingsley, apparently stubborn evidence of the moral bankruptcy of the antebellum mindset of white Christians is filtered through the political discourse of the time, influenced by perceived heterodoxies and their struggle for dominance within the overall propaganda framework of the slave-owning class. In this process, it becomes not counterevidence of the moral correctness of slavery but a confirmation of the correctness of one particular defense of slavery favored by the author.

Now that he understands that Salih Bilali is Fulani, Couper is free to divulge that on his plantation, many of his slaves are enslaved in a way that would strike most Southern whites as insufficiently authoritarian, with many of the enslaved Muslims especially living their lives in relative autonomy.

This certainly is not a typical arrangement for enslaved workers on all Sea Island plantations. Still, it is the case for at least one other group – the enslaved Muslims who work on Sapelo Island under Bilali Muhammad, who comes in for a very brief mention in Couper's letter. It is a minimal appearance, but it is a significant one as it is the first time someone managed to get Bilali's birthplace – Timbu, in modern Guinea – into the formal record.

So, while the direct evidence of Bilali's network of potential allies in preserving his legacy is somewhat scant, we can begin to understand many of the pressures Bilali's project was under and the tools that might have been available to him in pursuing it. He is in a part of the US where enslaved Muslims are commonly granted special privileges. That fact has emergent propaganda value in advancing the ideological interests of the local slave-owning class. He is also known to and respected by other Black Muslim leaders on other plantations.

Little is known of Bilali's last few decades of life between Hodgson's account of his acquaintance with Salih Bilali and Bilali's death in 1859. However, it is known through other sources that the Georgia Sea Islands were home to other self-deluded pro-slavery reformers with attitudes similar to those of Hodgson, Couper, and Kingsley.

Colonial Countermyth: Kemble's Journal and Abolitionism

The story of one such figure is instructive. Pierce Mease Butler (a likely historical antecedent of Rhett Butler from *Gone with the Wind*) had an ownership stake in various Sea Island plantations and regularly expressed misgivings about the brutality of the slave trade. He envisioned a system on his farms, which he had inherited from his grandfather, like the ones administered by Bilali Muhammad and Salih Bilali. Still, his white overseer Roswell King, Jr. had no interest in such ideas. King was a notoriously cruel and wanton man who routinely raped enslaved women under his charge.

For years Butler kept the true conditions at his plantations secret from his wife, the liberal Philadelphia actress Fannie Kemble and Butler's description reassured her of his idealized conception of slavery, also inherited from his grandfather, which included an easier life for the more civilized of the people he held in bondage. But eventually, Kemble insisted she be shown the actual conditions on the family plantations, and when Butler finally relented in 1839, what Kemble saw shocked and offended her. Particularly horrifying to her was the overtly sexual nature of the white domination of the island's black population, with enslaved women having no control over their bodies or wombs and men's worst sexual predilections allowed to run rampant. Kemble began producing radical abolitionist writing, which would eventually lead to her husband divorcing her, taking custody of their two children, and leaving her penniless.

To them, the survival of slavery as an institution depended on maintaining a robust philosophical and moral defense of slavery that must include at least some practical reforms. They believed sincerely that the Sea Island institution of slavery represented a gentler, more morally palatable form of slavery that had a chance to be accepted by the rest of the Union and forestall the coming crisis long enough for European Christians to convert Africa to Christianity and thus resolve the issue of slavery to everyone's mutual satisfaction.

At the time of his death, Bilali represented, in this framework, robust evidence that a better form of slavery was possible administered correctly under a system like the one proposed by Kingsley in which enslaved people were not one undifferentiated caste of black people, but a multilayered system in which only the least civilized – and thus most in need of the civilizing influence of the institution of Christian slavery – need be held in anything like the brutal bondage commonly associated with freshwater slavery.

Security and Obscurity: Goulding and the Bilali Document

Despite the advantages afforded his project by the structure of Sea Islands culture, Bilali's choice to entrust his writings to Francis Goulding, a famous children's author living on the mainland, rather than to anyone at the Sapelo Island plantation, seems to have been a wise one. The outbreak of the Civil War would have put Bilali's writings at risk in more ways than one.

As a matter of physical security, the Sea Islands would have been rugged for Bilali's *Meditations* once the Civil War broke out in 1861. The islands could not be adequately defended from the Federal Navy and were one of the first Southern outposts occupied by Union troops after the war. The white people on many of the plantations mainly had moved inland or fled Georgia entirely by 1863. St. Simons became a refugee camp, and the plantation economy on Sapelo Island disintegrated into subsistence farming communities of the formerly enslaved. It was not the sort of environment where written archives would have likely had much chance of being preserved.

Perhaps even more importantly, the breakup of the Union into a hot war between Southern slaveholding states and Northern non-slave states completely changed the political significance of Bilali and his manuscript. The outbreak of war diminished the status among Southern whites of ideas like Hodgson's and Kingsley's, thus robbing the manuscript of most, if not all, of the interest which the slave-owning class might have had in protecting and promoting its inclusion in the factual record. For them, Bilali's story had lost its relevance.

Whether by design or luck, Bilali could preserve his manuscript from these pitfalls by entrusting them to a wealthy white non-slave owner, the famous children's author and inventor Francis Goulding. Goulding, who had invented one of the first sewing machines and written the popular children's novel *The Young Marooners*, had an extensive library on the mainland where Bilali's *Meditations* sat safe and sound for many decades from Bilali's death in 1859, through Goulding's death in 1881, until finally in 1930 it was deposited in the Georgia State Library by Goulding's son.

Though *Meditations* was the only significant written work Bilali left behind, in no sense does that form the extent of his legacy to Geechee/Gullah culture. When he died, Bilali left behind a corpus of teaching stories, customs, and cultural practices, including songs and recipes that continued to be passed down by residents of the communities that remained on Sapelo Island in the aftermath of the end of slavery.

Reconstruction and the Great Migration

In the late 1870's the outlook for black people living in the Deep South gradually deteriorated as it became clear that the US government intended to default on the promise of Reconstruction. That process finally came to fruition in 1877 with the presidency of Rutherford B. Hayes, whose contested election had led to a compromise that returned formal control of the entire South to the Democratic machine, which in Georgia was dominated by plantation owners.

Although The Great Migration is generally said to have begun around the turn of the 20th century, in the Sea Islands, black communities had started to empty and migrate – both inland and to the north – long before, as their communities were sold off to investors and turned into game preserves for the wealthy.

Life on Sapelo Island did continue, however, and Bilali's central position in Sapelo culture remained. In interviews with those who lived on Sapelo during Reconstruction, many of whom claim descent from Bilali, Bilali's name invariably comes up. While people tended to be reluctant to discuss the ongoing practice of Islam on the island (a reluctance that I found when traveling to the island continues to this day), the picture painted of Bilali is of a devout Muslim scholar, teacher, and patriarch.

The major formal sources of information about Sapelo during Reconstruction are Lydia Parrish's *Slave Songs of the Georgia Sea Islands*, discussed in the next section, and *Drums and Shadows*, a Works Progress Administration writer's project from the 1920s in which writers conducted interviews with elderly residents of the Sea Islands. The book's focus on Hoodoo at the expense of other Geechee/Gullah religious culture elements is a bit unfortunate. Still, in the case of Katie Brown, Bilali's great-granddaughter by his wife Phoebe, she can eventually get across that Bilali and his descendants were practitioners of Islam.

Katie Brown's account provides a vital link between Bilali and Joel Chandler Harris' Ben Ali books – the animal teaching story. Though her story of the lizard and the rabbit does not itself appear in Harris' book, the form of the story makes clear that such stories did circulate on Sapelo among Bilali's descendants and provide essential support for emergent interpretations of these stories as representing something more significant than simple allegories of slave life.

Another key source confirming Bilali's central role in Geechee culture on Sapelo is Cornelia Walker Bailey and Christina Bledsoe's *God, Dr. Buzzard, and the Bolito Man*, a memoir of Bailey's life on Sapelo Island that begins with a scene of Bilali rolling out his prayer rug just before sunrise on the eastern beaches of the island. Although Bilali was long dead by the time any of the current accounts of life on Sapelo were written, it is apparent that the tradition of an Islamic patriarch who led prayers on the eastern beach of Sapelo morning, noon, and the evening continued for many generations after his passing.

Father of the Dust: Dash's Bilali as Geechee Patriarch

Julie Dash's film *Daughters of the Dust*, set in 1902, depicts this critical post-Reconstruction period in the form of a delegation of former residents of St. Simons Island "who are returning to attempt to convince their remaining family members to migrate inland." Dash's film, though fictional, is an essential perspective on time in history that, because of the lack of formal documentation of life in these communities, modern scholars may have difficulty visualizing. It is an artist's conception of the networks that would have preserved Bilali's legacy in the decades after his death but before his manuscript was rediscovered, not only in Sea Islands culture but in the Geechee/Gullah diaspora.

Watching this film in the modern-day, I am struck by how closely it maps onto elements of Bilali's project, which my mind has never before had the organs of perception to contemplate. The film opens just as *God, Dr. Buzzard, and the Bolito Man* do, at sunrise on the Georgia Sea Islands in 1902, with a shot of a man reading an Arabic document and singing the Islamic call to prayer.

It is not until the film's final quarter that any more mention is made of Bilali or Islam. Instead, Dash first picks up the story of the delegation above, which is evocative of a troupe of mourners attending a funeral for the island. Viola, the Christian missionary, carries with her the promise of civilization and respectability in a steady mainland culture if reluctantly, carving out a place in society for black people who can sincerely express faith in Christianity and renounce other beliefs spiritual practices.

There is the free spirit Yellow Mary, who carries with her the promise of urban modernity, leaving behind the trappings of their defunct lives under the racist oppression of postbellum southern culture and moving on without memory of the trauma of history. Yellow Mary eventually chooses to stay on the island with Nana Peazant, breaking her lover Trula's heart.

Still living on the island is Eula, pregnant perhaps by her husband Eli and perhaps by her white rapist and their Unborn Child, who serves as one of the film's narrators. They carry with them the promise of the future itself, uncertain and full of anguish but also containing a small yet credible message of hope.

Haagar, Eula's sister, cherishes the promise of economic prosperity through skilled work on the mainland. Still, her daughter's love affair with a Cherokee man calls into question the costs of leaving behind the family's ancestral home. Binding them all together is the matriarch and fount of mother-wit Nana Peazant, who carries the songs, recipes, and wisdom of living Geechee/Gullah culture.

After the dynamics of these characters' relationships play out in a series of remembrances and commentaries, in the film's final quarter Bilali appears on the screen. Still, like so many of the elements of Dash's film, his appearance raises far more questions than it answers. This Bilali cannot be the historical Bilali, and it is unclear if he represents an actual historical figure. However, the man may be intended to be Bilali Muhammad's (or Salih Bilali's) son. Even the character's origins seem mysterious – perhaps Africa, perhaps the Caribbean. Yet, there is some connection. The threefold placement of Bilali in the film, praying at sunrise in the first shot, again praying at dawn in the final image, and telling his own story directly after Nana Peazant's crucial speech about how there must be a connection between the people of the island, the people who have migrated north, and the people back in Africa, suggest a continuing centrality of Islam in Georgia Sea Islands culture. Still, the essential role of Islam in life on the island in 1902 remains almost entirely opaque.

The knowledge only deepens the mystery that at the moment his culture is enduring this reckoning, Bilali himself is for the most part unknown to the broader culture, his manuscript still sitting unnoticed in the library Captain Goulding had willed to his son in 1881. Indeed, when the sun sets on the still-unresolved tensions among the Peazant clan in 1902, Bilali's *Meditations* will not be heard again for almost thirty more years.

The Myth of Ben Ali: Charles Goulding's Affidavit

Geechee/Gullah culture spread to most country areas with significant black populations throughout these decades, becoming one of the more prominent and more influential creole Diasporas in the 20th century United States. Though unknown in the mainstream US culture, Bilali was revered throughout the Geechee/Gullah diaspora as a critical ancestral teaching figure.

The name of one Geechee/Gullah woman who took the stories, songs, and recipes of the Sea Islands north to Philadelphia seems to be unknown to history at this time. However, she indeed went to work in the childhood home of Lydia Austin, who remembered the songs the woman sang to her when Austin was growing up in a Quaker family in Salem County, New Jersey, in the late 1800s.

When Austin, by then Lydia Parrish and the wife of renowned painter Maxfield Parrish, traveled to St. Simons in 1915, she heard Julie Armstrong singing a song that she recognized from the Geechee/Gullah songs. The two became friends, and Parrish devoted the subsequent decades of her life to preserving and furthering the culture that remained there.

In the process, she collected a bit of information about Bilali, but most of the biographical details she learned seem to be reflected to some degree in previous accounts. In furthering Bilali's project, she was instrumental. While Lydia Parrish was carefully preserving and chronicling the living Geechee/Gullah culture, Francis Goulding's son was slowly becoming aware that he may have something of great value indeed in his father's dusty old library. In 1930, the younger Goulding showed up at the Georgia State Library with the manuscript in hand. He was adamant that he gave an affidavit certifying his account of the manuscript's contents as the official record thereof. The library obliged him.

Ronald Judy was the first modern scholar to take up a severe interrogation of what was going on in Goulding's strange insistence on creating an official document describing what he called *The Diary of Ben Ali*. Judy wrote his *(Dis)Informing the American Canon* in 1993 before Muhammad al-Ahari's updated translation of *Meditations* would have allowed him to definitively answer the question of whether Goulding's account of what was in the document is accurate, although Judy is appropriately skeptical. We know now that it was unquestionably not accurate.

The document Goulding was swearing to the contents was utterly opaque to him – he had no idea of what it said. He hoped that it would one day prove to be a supporting material for the work of Joel Chandler Harris, a famous author who had written about a character who seemed similar to the man who had passed the manuscript to his father. Harris had published two children's books in the late 1890s that drew upon the story of the historical Bilali Muhammad to create the fictional character of Aaron, Son of Ben Ali, and Harris claimed that this Ben Ali had left behind a diary written in a desert dialect. This was apparently enough to cause Goulding to imagine that the book in his father's library was indeed the diary Harris was referencing.

The most significant impact of Goulding's disinformation was that for most of the 20th century, the official story of Bilali Muhammad was that he was a white Arab slave trader named Ben Ali. He had worked on Sapelo Island as an overseer. The impact on Bilali's eventual legacy was not quite decisive, but it caused an extraordinary amount of confusion in the formal literature for many years.

Bilali in Flight: Lydia Parrish to Toni Morrison and Beyond

Less than a decade before the manuscript was discovered by far more beneficent custodian – Lydia Parrish. During her research for *Slave Songs of the*

Georgia Sea Islands, Parrish learned of the document's existence and rushed to the library to see it and read Goulding's affidavit.

Goulding's misinformation excited Parrish because it seemed to her that if Goulding's account were valid, the diary would contain confirmation of much of the information she had been gathering over the previous twenty-five years of her life. The discovery of a diary of a man who lived and worked as a founding patriarch of the culture she was laboring to help preserve must have seemed too good to be true, and Parrish would discover that it was not likely true at all.

She sent a Photostat copy of the manuscript to Melville Herskovitz, one of the most important early 20th-century anthropologists of black culture in the Americas. In a sense, Herskovitz was the perfect choice for the project, having just finished *Life in a Haitian Valley,* he would have been in a uniquely advantageous position to undertake the task of situating Bilali's vision of Sea Island Islam in the context of the other cultural forces at work on the island such as mainline Christianity, Quakerism, and other West African religions besides Islam.

Unfortunately for Parrish, Herskovitz was in the process of getting his book to publication and also starting up the Anthropology Department at Northwestern when he received the manuscript and had no time to investigate it personally. Instead, he passed it along to Joseph Greenberg, who traveled to Africa to see what he could learn of the document.

It is known today that much of what Greenberg discovered was reasonably accurate or close enough to illuminate, but his methods did not inspire much confidence in his conclusions. Unaware that Bilali was from Timbu, Greenberg traveled to a different part of Africa. The Muslim scholars (who could at least read Arabic) told him that Bilali was barely literate and was probably trying to recreate the Risalah of Ibn Abi-Zayd. Once Greenberg told Lydia Parrish that the diary was a Muslim religious document, Lydia Parrish did little else to develop the manuscript or promote its understanding by scholars. It would be more than fifty years before Bilali Muhammad would again catch the eye of historians to any significant degree.

al-Ahari gives credit to Greenberg, who, in dispelling or at least calling into question Goulding's original inaccurate account of "The Diary of Ben Ali," made an essential contribution to furthering Bilali's legacy. But he also makes clear that Greenberg's conclusions were likely also incorrect, as Bilali was not simply trying to reproduce from memory something he remembered from childhood. Bilali's *Meditations* is a proper Islamic legal document and an original composition of Bilali Muhammad. This makes the document somewhat tricky, if not impossible, for modern translators to understand fully.

Through painstaking effort, al-Ahari and other scholars have been able to translate most of what Bilali wrote and come to a complete understanding of Bilali's Sapelo Island traditions. More important than any new translation of *Meditations* is that beginning in 1977, Bilali himself and the body of knowledge he represents, through the continued advance of black novelists and directors steeped in Bilali lore, has begun appearing in the mainstream culture more and more, beginning with Toni Morrison's National Book Award-winning *Song of Solomon* and then in Dash's *Daughters of the Dust* which in 2004 was selected for inclusion in The National Registry of Film. Against incredible odds (though also with great help from a robust network of allies), it would seem that Bilali, his community, and their descendants have successfully written themselves, their culture, and their legacy into being.

Conclusion

It is important not to lose sight, as Bilali's *Meditations* finally finds its way into the formal literature in a way that lays to rest many of the mysteries that once surrounded it, that Bilali's legacy persists not only in his ancient writings but also in a living culture that continues and thrives to this day. Nor can those who value Bilali and his work become complacent at the apparent ascendancy of his legacy. Bilali's history is a stark lesson in the perils that beset stories like Bilali's in a world where concerted attempts have been made over centuries to distort, exclude and delegitimize stories of West African Islam in the Americas. A story can seem ascendant one moment, only to fall into dormancy and obscurity for decades and longer if it falls out of favor with the dominant intellectual culture.

To participate in and further the work of Bilali and those like him, it is necessary to transcend the boundaries of various academic disciplines and experience, as best as we are able, in the preservation and furthering of cultures like the one he left behind when he died on Sapelo Island in 1859. Historical narratives pick up and leave off, as do references to Bilali in the literary canon, as do appearances of Bilali stories and songs in the dominant cultural history. Only by drawing together these disparate sources can we truly hear Bilali's music and ensure that this uniquely American hymn can continue to be sung by many generations in the future.

Work Cited

al-Ahari, Muhammed Abdullah. *Bilali Muhammad: Muslim Jurisprudist in Antebellum Georgia*. Magribine, 2010. Print.

Austin, Allan D. "Bilali Mohammed and Salih Bilali." *African Muslims in Antebellum America, Transatlantic Stories and Spiritual Struggles*. Routledge, 1997. Print.

Dabovic, Safet. "Displacement and the Negotiation of an American Identity in African Muslim Slave Narratives." Diss. Stonybrook University, 2009. Print.

Daughters of the Dust. Dir. Julie Dash. Prod. Julie Dash. By Julie Dash. Perf. Adisa Anderson and Vertamae Smart-Grosvenor. Kino International, 1992. Film.

Fleszar, Mark J. *The Atlantic Mind: Zephaniah Kingsley, Slavery, and the Politics of Race in the Atlantic World.* Diss. Georgia State University, 2009. Print.

Finlayson, Lorna. *The Political Is Political: Conformity and the Illusion of Dissent in Contemporary Political Philosophy.* Rowman & Littlefield International, 2015. Print.

Hodgson, William. *Notes on Northern Africa, the Sahara, and Soudan.* New York, 1844. Print.

Kingsley, Zephaniah. *Treatise on the Patriarchal, or Cooperative System of Society.* Ithaca, 1828. Print.

López, Ian Haney. *White by Law 10th Anniversary Edition: The Legal Construction of Race.* New York University Press, 2006. Print.

Ware, Rudolph. *The Walking Qu'ran: Islamic Education, Embodied Knowledge, and History in West Africa.* The University of North Carolina Press, 2014. Print.

Chapter 6

Beyond Western Eyes: Theorizing Feminism in the Indian Context

Chandrakala Padia

Professor,
Department of Political Science,
Banaras Hindu University, Varanasi

Abstract

The present chapter makes an effort to generate a counter-argument of Western Feminism as Indian Feminism. The various forms of Eurocentric biases towards Western feminist narratives have strategically prevented the rise of the phenomenon of Indian Feminism. It is important to note that there is no dearth of indigenous theoretical and philosophical thinking in India. But, what has mostly happened is the indigenous phenomena have been subject to distortions and misinterpretations. In collaboration with the Western-educated Indian scholars, Western scholars mistranslated and mis-transcreated the conceptual foundations of the diverse indigenous feminist practices in India in such a manner that they continue to be acknowledged in contemporary India. Today this can be categorically observed through family practices, institutional functional patterns, syllabus structures, media portrayals, etc. With respect to these arguments at the backdrop, this chapter unpacks the various socio-historical narratives associated with the phenomena of Indian Feminism from diverse ancient Hindu religio-philosophical texts and scriptures.

Keywords: Eurocentric, Western Feminism, mistranslated, Indian Feminism, religio-philosophical

* * *

Introduction

The present chapter is an attempt to construct an Indian theory of feminism. It tries to project how due to the ethnocentric and Eurocentric biases present in Western Feminist discourse, an Indian theory of feminism could not be evolved. However, there is no shortage of literary and sociological writings in

India's classical and modern languages. It also uncovers the misreading of Indian ancient texts by many Western and Indian scholars and shows how these scholars have misunderstood the conceptual foundations of these texts and have distorted the meaning of *parampara* in the Indian worldview, resulting in false representations of Indian Women and their limited understanding of Sanskrit language. To a great extent wrong translations of Indian classical texts have led to the justification of many unhealthy practices in Indian society.

Though the Western Feminist thought dominates contemporary feminist discourse today, yet it suffers from deep-seated ethnocentric and Eurocentric biases. Scholars have studied and analyzed the Indian reality through some borrowed Western Models. This has come in the way of constructing an Indian theory of feminism. Despite the rich corpus of literary and sociological writings in our languages—classical and modern—on issues related to women, there has been no concerted attempt to construct an Indian theory of feminism. There exist Black feminism, American and French Schools of feminism but no Indian School of feminism as such. The reason lies in the fact that Indian academia has either ignored the Indian tradition and relied on Western epistemological models or has relied on western interpretations of Indian texts/conditions.

This blanket following the West, colonial mindset, and scant attention to our traditions and culture have perpetuated the misreading of our ancient texts, misinterpretation of their conceptual foundations, distortion of the meaning of *parampara*, and identification of modernity, Westernization and progress, and the construction of several binaries. Within such a framework, women are supposed to be emancipated only through Western economic rationality, where there is no place for historically informed and culturally specific analysis. Such a notion of women's emancipation has some severe implications that lead to the emergence of three false representations of Third World women.

In the first representation, the Western feminists have subconsciously internalized the demeaning images of Indian and Third World cultures to the total neglect of their positive aspects. There are numerous examples of such representations. In her *Bananas Beaches and Base: Making Feminist Sense of International Politics*, Enloe writes about veiled third world women as "mindless members of a harem, preoccupied with petty domestic rivalries rather than with artistic and political affairs of their times" (53). In this presentation, the public-private dichotomy is projected in the same way as that of the West but with a double standard of colonial hierarchy. Western women are deemed superior, while Third World women are treated as oblivious to the real world and inferior to Western women because Western women do not wear a veil.

In the second representation, Third World women are shown as sex objects. As Spivak observes, "Third World women are not allowed to speak" and are "deeply in the shadow" (237). Thus, colonization is justified as a benign and paternalistic attitude of the colonizer rather than being acknowledged as a subjugating and exploiting practice.

In the third representation, Western feminists and feminist writings often portray Third World women as victims. These feminists claim to know the shared and gendered oppression of women. In so doing, they misrepresent the varied interest of different women by homogenizing the experiences and conditions of Western women across time and culture. Chandra Talpade Mohanty argues that such a monolithic and singular portrayal of Third World women as victims of modernization, of undifferentiated patriarchy, and male domination produce reductive understandings of "Third World women's multiple realities" (333-34).

Third World women are discursively created separate and distant from the historical, socio-political, and lived material realities of their existence in all three representations. They share the implicit assumption that Third World women are traditional, non-liberated, and need to be civilized and developed, i.e., more like Western women.

Further, there has been no effort to understand Indian reality in a socio-historic-cultural context. To illustrate, the forms of violence against the Third World women, such as dowry murders get represented in the West as instances of death by culture. In contrast, analogous forms of violence in Western contexts, such as domestic brutality and murders, have been regarded as merely episodic. Trinh T. Minh-ha has pointed out that such an approach fails to be sympathetic to cultural differences and so tends to prescribe a kind of apartheid policy of separate development which may be put thus: "keep your way of life and ethnic values within the borders of your homelands" (80). Such a misreading of cultures arises because most of the Western scholars have adopted an anthropological perspective to culture. This way of looking rests on the analysis of cultures merely based on outward modes of living such as dress and food habits, etc., and it is precisely this perspective that shapes most feminist approaches to the third world today. As a result, speaking of culture in general, Western culture either totally excludes or marginalizes third world culture or is unsympathetic to other cultures as it has always based its understanding of these cultures not on what they are but only on their representations, replete with unduly negative stereotypes and imputations of cultural inferiority.

On the one hand, they prefer to adopt, condescendingly, a benevolent attitude by taking special care to insist that third world women be represented in feminist writings; on the other, they exhibit a strong tendency to visualize all women merely based on the feminine figure and other external features, ignoring the unseen but essential difference of value-sense and cultural traditions. This is why many third-world feminist scholars argue that if their women are to be liberated, they must raise their voices against the essentialist construction of third-world women, Universalist assumptions of sexist oppression across different cultures, and binary structures of modernity versus tradition.

Investigating the Patriarchal Past

In the Indian context, no importance is accorded to the learning of Sanskrit as a key to the understanding of our sociological texts resulting in misrepresentation of these texts both by the Western and Indian scholars. It needs to be elaborated how this has led the people of both North and South to have a distorted and fabricated understanding of our texts. A few examples can be cited in support of the above argument. One of the most glaring examples is that of one of the Verses of *Ṛg Veda Samhita*. In September 1987, an eighteen-year-old woman, Roop Kanwar, immolated herself in the name of *sati*; many modern Indian writers claimed that this *sati pratha* had the sanction of the *Vedas*. In support of this claim, they cited a hymn from the *Ṛg Veda Samhita*, which requires the widow to sit within the fire that burns her dead husband's body:

imā nārīravidhavāḥ supatnīrāñjanena sarpiṣā saṁ viśantu |

anaśravo'namīvāḥ suratnā ā rohantu janayo yonimagre ||

(*Ṛg Veda* 7)

This verse has been misread as - may these very good and holy women devoted to their husbands enter fire together with the husband's body. However, Vedic scholars later proved that this reading of the hymn is based on an orthographic mistake. The significant word is *agre* (in front), not *agne* (O, Agni). Even if we accept the reading *agne*, it would not mean into the fire, for the word would still be in the vocative case and signify that *agni* was being addressed. The sense of into the fire would be yielded only if the word were in the dative case, *agnaye*. P. V. Kane claims that the verse has been presented in a corrupted form because the interpreters probably read the last quarter of *Ṛg Veda Samhita* as *arohantujalayonim-agne* (let them ascend the watery seat or origin, O, fire!) meaning "may fire be to them as cool as water" (25). All other verses clarify that either the hymn directs the widow to sit facing her dead husband; or that this *mantra* was not addressed to widows but to ladies of the deceased man's household whose husbands were living.

However, the point that the disputed *Ṛg Veda* verse can never be interpreted as requiring the widow to die with her husband becomes clearer when one reads the very next verse. Here, the wife is directed to accept her loving husband's death quietly, arise from her husband's side, and resume her place in the world:

udīrṣva nāryabhi jīvalokaṁ gatāsumetamupa śeṣa ehi |

hastagrābhasya didhiṣostavedaṁ patyurjanitvamabhi saṁ babhūtha ||

(*Ṛg Veda* 18)

It is imperative to understand the Indian worldview for constructing an Indian theory of feminism. India's intellectual tradition accepts man and woman as equals. The *Ṛg Veda Samhita* agrees with a common source of all living beings, i.e., one Will manifesting itself in many forms, including the male and the female in the *Nasadiya Sukta*.

nāsadāsīnno sadāsīttadānīṁ nāsīdrajo no vyomā paro yat |

kimāvarīvaḥ kuha kasya śarmannambhaḥ kimāsīdgahanaṁ gabhīram ||

(*Ṛg Veda* 10)

na mṛtyurāsīdamṛtaṁ na tarhi na rātryā ahna āsītpraketaḥ |

ānīdavātaṁ svadhayā tadekaṁ tasmāddhānyanna paraḥ kiṁ canāsa ||

(*Ṛg Veda* 12)

Manusmriti also subscribes to the same viewpoint. It says:

dvidhā kṛtvā'tmano dehamardhena

puruṣo'bhavat |

ardhena nārī tasyāṁ sa virājamasṛjat prabhuḥ ||

(Manu 32)

This concept of *Shakti* is unique to Indian philosophy. It may have been the tradition in the West to equate power with masculine nature. Still, the Indian worldview offers a radically different approach in the concept of *Shakti*, where one discovers the idea of the feminine as being the very manifestation of power itself. The respect for *Shakti* in Hinduism is not limited to the religion's literary heritage only. The same word *Shakti* itself appears twelve times in the *Ṛg Veda*

Samhita. Part of the *Ṛg Veda Samhita* is known as the *Devi Sukta* (tenth canto of the *Ṛg Veda Samhita*) and is undoubtedly recognition of *Shakti* as a cosmic principle. The various schools of Vedic philosophy *(shad-darshanas)* also took this principle quite seriously. For the Vedanta school, *Shakti* was conceived as the activity of the cause revealing itself in the shape of an effect. The *Naiyayika* logicians attempted to explain *Shakti* in terms of being the function or property of a reason. The *Mimamskaras* held that *Shakti* was no less than the inherent power of all things. *Samkhya* is the most influential school in formulating a theory of *Shakti.* It teaches the dualistic doctrine of *Prakriti/Purusha.* According to this theory, there are two radically different principles at play during the creations of the Cosmos: matter (*Prakriti*) and spirit (*Purusha*). *Prakriti* is the primordial matter which is present before the cosmos becomes manifest. As a direct result of the devolution of this original material substance, the universe, with all its diversity of names and forms, comes into being. *Prakriti* is seen as being the power of nature, both animate and inanimate as such nature is seen as dynamic energy.

Here, every woman is said to be a manifestation of the divine *Shakti.* The power of *Shakti* is believed to be directly present in creation in the form of our mothers, sisters, daughter, and wives. In this context, contemporary feminist scholar Elinor Gadon comments:

> The truth of the Goddess is the mystery of our being. She is the dynamic life force within. Her form is embedded in our collective psyche, part of what it is to be human. She is the dance of life, and her song is eros, the energy of creation. That said, however, because the menstrual form of feminine bravery has been so marginalized (virtually made invisible) throughout Western civilization's progress, there must be the extra responsibility placed on male authors (especially) of the heroic, to come to terms with their more than half of the distortion and pathology of inherent heroism-narcissism. (131)

Elinor Gadon admits that she was frustrated by a lack of imagery that resonated with her ideal of womanhood. When she traveled to Calcutta in 1967 with her family, she realized how much she had missed. "Being in a culture so utterly different from my own, the feminine was celebrated everywhere in sensuous images of great power both human and divine, was profoundly unsettling" (120). Western-oriented religions have a shortage of female-oriented imagery and symbolism, in contrast to Eastern religions such as Hinduism. Unlike Western literature, Indian literature is full of accounts of heroic, strong, and brave women. For example, Draupadi in *Mahabharata* is depicted as a bold and iron-willed woman. As the mother of Pandavas, Kunti is a lady of immense courage who keeps her honor and faith intact despite a life full of tragedies. In the *Ramayana,* Sita emerges as a powerful woman who chooses her husband who breaks the most powerful *dhanush* (bow) of Mahadev, accompanies Rama to the forest against her in-laws' will, thus exhibits her strength throughout. There are also living historical records of India where Hindu women have historically quickly risen to heights of power within various monastic and religious hierarchical structures, parallels of which would have been unheard of in Western religion and society until only recently. Klaus Klostermaier, the famous historian, in his article *Sri Tattva* claims that in the earliest Vedic era, "women were awarded the sacred thread of the *brahmanas*" (Klostermaier 21-36). One text of the *Ṛg Veda Samhita* mentions a female *rishi,* or revealer of sacred truth, known as Vishvara. There were also women philosophers such as Vachaknavi, who debated *Yajnavalkya,* of *Upanishadic* fame. The famous Sanskrit grammarian *Panini* observed that the distinction in the Sanskrit language between *Acaryani* (the wife of a teacher) and *Acaryaa* (a lady teacher) indicated that women were accepted as spiritual teachers. Women saints such as Andal and Mirabai were leaders of the devotional Bhakti movements that initiated the religious liberation of women and were largely promoted and supported by women devotees. Women have continued this ancient tradition as leaders of various Hindu communities to this day. Such examples can be found in the forms of Gurumayi Chidvilasananda, Amritanandamayi, and Meera Ma, among many others. Considering that Indian culture has invariably been a culture in which religion has always been the most important social institution in society, it is no small accomplishment for women to have risen so high in the echelons of Hindu leadership.

There has been generated a false belief about women having a subservient status in Indian sociological texts. Most scholars have adopted an alien methodology that projects the complex, inter-related, and multiple realities of India as simple facts undermining the significance of the Indian worldview and its distinctiveness compared to the Western worldview. An in-depth analysis of the Indian worldview answers the ethnocentric and Eurocentric nature of Western feminism. It would be appropriate to discuss them one by one.

Simone de Beauvoir, in her seminal work *Second Sex* claims that "it is the whole process by which femininity is manufactured in society" (50-53). She is defined and differentiated regarding man and not about her; she is incidental, the inessential as opposed to the essential. What Simone de Beauvoir claims in her work is valid only about Western feminism. In the Indian context, women enjoy the freedom to choose their careers, be it *brahmacharinis* or *grihastha* women. They were never treated as incidental, inessential, or have never been defined regarding man. Instead, it is the name of a woman who always comes first, such as *Sita-Ram, Radhe-Krishna, Lakshmi-Ganesh,* etc. The women were not only equal to men but were accorded a superior position. The ancient texts are full of such verses. See the following quote:

uta tvā strī śaśīyasī puṁso bhavati vasyasī |

adevatrādarādhasaḥ ||

[...many a woman is more steadfast and better than the man who turns away from God ... and does not offer prayers].

(Ṛg Veda 61)

Manu unequivocally assigns to women the status of presiding deities in the home. According to him, there is no difference whatsoever between wives who are destined to bear children and who provide the blessings of love and caring and those idols put in the houses of men for worship as symbols of good fortune and holiness:

prajanārthaṃ mahābhāgāḥ pūjārhā gṛhadīptayaḥ |

striyaḥ śriyaśca geheṣu na viśeṣo'sti kaścana ||

(Manu 26)

The *Mahābhārata* looks at the woman as the pre-eminent source of family happiness. What is more, the *Mahābhārata* looks at women as the anchor not only of family life but of the social organism. The very future of a country depends on women, essentially because they beget and nurture children and impart the proper *samskaras* (or value-based dispositions) to them.

Manu says: "One *ācārya* surpasses ten ordinary teachers; one father surpasses one hundred *āchāryas*; and above all, one mother surpasses a thousand fathers."

upādhyāyān daśācārya ācāryāṇāṃ śataṃ pitā |

sahasraṃ tu pitṝn mātā gauraveṇātiricyate ||

(Manu 145)

Simone de Beauvoir refers to many great Western thinkers who have assigned women a derogatory status. Plato, in his *Laws*, declares that women are "by nature" (781) at least twice as bad as men. Aristotle outdoes even Plato in denigrating women. He turns the thesis of the comparative inferiority of women into a justification of her general domination by men. Aristotle's teleological theory of reality believes that its final cause determines each individual's growth, that is, by what it is to become at the end. Thus, a seed develops into a tree and a child into a grown-up human being. Likewise, a girl realizes her full significance as a female in becoming a mother, that is, by participating in the function of reproduction. But in so doing, a woman, according to Aristotle, is only a passive recipient; she only provides matter to the process of reproduction, and the father offers the imprint of human personality on this matter. Man is the active agent; that is why; he may be regarded as superior to women. See the following quote of Aristotle:

> Since the Form is *better* and more divine in its nature than the Matter, it is *better* also that the superior one should be separate from the inferior one. That is why, whenever possible and so far as possible, the male is separate from the female. A woman is "as it were an infertile male," and even in regard to reproduction, a male is male in virtue of particular ability and a female in virtue of a particular inability. (*Generation* 766)

Many other details of Aristotle's views on women are full of derogatory remarks. See the following:

> Virtues and actions are nobler when they proceed from those who are naturally worthier, for instance, from a man rather than from a woman. (*Politics I* 1367)

Consider the following quote again from Aristotle's *The Art of Rhetoric:*

> They must all share in (moral goodness), but not in the same way—each sharing only to the extent required for the discharge of his or her function. The ruler, accordingly, must possess moral goodness in *its full* or *perfect* form because his function demands a master-artificer, and the reason is such a *master artificer;* but *all other* persons need only possess moral goodness *to the extent* required of them. It is thus clear that temperance and similarly fortitude and justice *are not,* as Socrates held, the *same* in a woman as they are in a man. Fortitude in the one, for example, is shown in connection with the ruling; in the other, it is shown in connection with serving; and the same is true of the other forms of goodness. To speak in general terms, and to maintain that goodness consists in "a good condition of the soul" or in "right action" or in anything of the kind, is to be guilty of self-deception. Far better than such general definitions is the method of simple enumeration of the different forms of goodness. (*The Art* 1260)

Even Rousseau's attitude to a woman is just as uncharitable, which is surprising because he is supposed to place a great deal of emphasis on *equality.* He defines a woman's nature in terms of her function—her sexual and procreative purposes in life. On the other hand, man has, according to him, limitless potential for rational thought and creativity. Consider in this context, the following statement of Rousseau:

> ...it is not enough that a wife should be faithful; her husband, along with his friends and neighbors, must believe in her fidelity ... Nature herself has decreed that woman, both for herself and her children, should be at the mercy of man's judgment ... Worth alone will not suffice, a woman must be *thought-worthy;* nor beauty, she must be *admired;* nor virtue, she must be *respected* ... "What will, people think" is the grave of a man's virtue and the throne of a woman's. (325-8)

Unfortunately, even a great philosopher like Hegel cannot see the possibility of exceptional qualities in women. Hegel develops a similar argument in his book *The Philosophy of Right:*

> The difference in the physical characteristics of the two sexes has a rational basis and consequently acquires an intellectual and ethical significance. This significance is determined by the difference into which the ethical substantiveness as the concept internally sunders itself in order that its vitality may become a concrete unity consequent upon this difference. Thus, one sex is mind in its self-diremption into explicit personal self-subsistence and the knowledge and volition of free universality, i.e., the self-consciousness of conceptual thought and the volition of the objective end. The other sex is the mind maintaining itself in unity, as knowledge and volition of the substantive, but knowledge and volition in the form of concrete individuality and feeling. Concerning externality, the former is powerful and active; the latter is passive and subjective. (144)

Hegel continues:

> Women are capable of education, but they are not made for activities that demand a universal faculty, such as the more advanced sciences, philosophy, and certain forms of artistic production. Women may have happy ideas, tastes, and elegance, but they cannot attain the ideal. The difference between men and women is like that between animals and plants. Men correspond to animals, while women correspond to plants because their development is more placid, and the principle that

underlies it is the rather vague unity of feeling. When women hold the helm of government, the stale is at once in jeopardy because women regulate their actions not by the demands of universality but by arbitrary inclinations and opinions. (263-64)

The underlying idea that resonates most clearly in our essential philosophical tradition is that a person is not only an individual among other individuals but is, in principle, knit indissolubly with a family, a community, and ultimately with the whole human race. This is why we have never looked at society as a mere aggregate of individuals but rather as a living organism where everyone complements the other and therefore helps create, sustain, and reinforce an evolved social order.

Indian Feminism: Beyond the European/Colonial Gaze

Now, the question that arises is how we can distinguish Indian Feminism from Western Feminism? To my mind, Indian feminism is distinct from Western feminism in following ways:

a. It does not believe in the dominant masculinist view of rationality, the sharp disjunction between reason and feeling, the equation of rationality with impersonality, justice with abstract impartiality, and equality with uniformity.

b. It recognizes concrete modes of difference, indigenous knowledge, and local expertise.

c. It critiques Western feminist discourses for presenting a monolithic category of women, Universalist assumptions of sexist operation across cultures, and finally, colonist intentions of such a discourse.

d. It never looks at society as a mere aggregate of individuals but rather as a living organism where everyone complements the other. It does not believe in normative dualism. Different roles are assigned to various persons following their nature and aptitude. There is no place here for the Utopia of a wholly independent and self-sufficing individual. The dominant emphasis has always been on the collective social interdependence. Superficially, this may seem to be oppressive, undemocratic. Still, in practice, such a view makes for promoting social cohesion and stability and an overall improvement in the quality of life. In the hierarchy of a social structure so conceived, the so-called subordinates and superiors have both been allotted specific and socially helpful functions. The former gets a chance to cultivate deference, loyalty, and obedience reasonably, and the latter to develop the attitudes of nurturance and concern so that the subordinates' capacity for self-effort may not be harmed.

e. It derives its basic premise from that cultural tradition that advocates an integrated working of the body, mind, and spirit, without which attaining the ultimate end of life is impossible. It is pretty different from the predominantly material civilization of the West today. By and large, the emphasis has been on the need to rise to a fuller vision of the Eternal by following the dictates of conscience, morality and *dharma*, and higher psychological practices. Our social system, in principle, is directed to this end. This is to be seen not only in our most ancient scriptures and books of knowledge like the *Vedas* and the *Upaniṣads* but in the *Smritis*, which are products of a much later period. To quote *Manusmṛiti*:

> sarvamātmani sampaśyet satcāsatca samāhitaḥ |
>
> sarvaṃ hyātmani sampaśyannādharme kurute manaḥ ||
>
> (Manu 118)

[Let man discriminate between good and evil, right and wrong, true and false, the real and the unreal; and thus determining, let him yet one-pointedly ever behold everything in the Self, the transitory as well as that which abides. He who beholdeth all in the Self his mind strayeth not into sin].

Further, the conceptual foundation of Indian feminism is rooted in the belief that culture is the primary determinant of consciousness. Any community is not a mere assemblage of parts but grows out of a long development of certain institutions and practices of the rule of law, authorities of equal respect, habits of common deliberation, common association, cultural action, and so on. Cultures are psychological creations of their relevant communities and products of their unique historical experiences as distilled and interpreted over centuries by their amazing imaginations. Every culture has a built-in capacity to reject some of its premises and adopt the new ones. This is what we mean by *parampara*.

f. Indian feminism, therefore, draws its source from the idea that our life is a part of larger cosmic order and not one of unencumbered, pure, self-defining subjectivity. It believes in collective, communicative, affective, spiritual orientations than individualistic, calculative, contractarian values. It believes in substantive rationality and not in technological rationality.

Freedom in the western sense of the term can never be a core value of Indian feminism. Indian Feminism does not believe in liberating oneself from the ties of family, community, and nation. It believes in cooperation, not in competition, inter-dependence, not in autonomy, and in sustaining nature, not in dominating. This is the reason that Indian feminism believes in the concept of *Ardhanarishwar* and *Sahdharmini*.

Now, what steps need to be taken to construct an Indian Theory of Feminism? The first and foremost need is to oppose the monolithic and singular portrayal of Indian women as victims of modernization, of undifferentiated patriarchy, and of reductive understanding of multiple realities of Indian women, the rejection of the implicit assumption of the feminist discourse in the West that Indian women were traditional, non-liberated, and need to be civilized and developed like Western women. The words of Sen and Grown can be quoted here to substantiate the above argument:

> Feminism cannot be monolithic in its issues, goals, and strategies since it constitutes the political expressions of the concerns of women from different regions, classes, nationalities, and ethnic backgrounds. There is and must be a diversity of feminisms, responsive to the different needs and concerns of different women and defined by them for themselves. This diversity builds on a common opposition to gender oppression and hierarchy. (18-19)

Secondly, Indian feminists are advised to be critical of homogenizing universalism and homogenizing differentials. There is a need to challenge the false understanding of experience, subjectivity, identity, and consciousness. What is needed is a theory of feminism based on performance rather than justification, verification, and control. At the same time, we need to successfully reveal the sexist assumptions and power structures embodied in literary texts, political treatises, and historical documents.

The scholars should adopt a methodology that tries to analyze every thesis based on three parameters: First, what is the speaker's status? Second, in whose name is the argument from the culture advanced? And third, what is the degree of participation in the cultural formation of the social groups primarily affected by the artistic practice in question?

It is only then that it will be possible to counter the Eurocentric nature of feminist thought. It would be pertinent to remember what bell hooks said in 20th-century political discourse–the term women are synonymous with white women, and the term blacks as synonymous with black men. Third-world women should not forget that their lived experiences shape their consciousness so that their worldview differs from those who have a degree of privilege. They must recognize that their marginality gives them a unique vantage point that they can use to criticize the dominant racist and sexist hegemony and envision and create counter-hegemony.

Conclusion

Based on the quotes and verses mentioned in India's ancient texts, it can be understood that gender discrimination is not a ubiquitous feature of Indian thought, which believes that genius abides in the soul, not in the bodily frame. So, there is no ground for preferring man to woman. As against Western Feminism, it rejects the dominant masculinist view of rationality, the sharp disjunction between reason and feeling, and the identification of equality with uniformity. Indian feminism believes in the concept of *Ardhanarishwar* (God as half man and half woman) and *Sahadharmini* (woman as an equal partner of her husband in all religious activities). An in-depth reading of ancient Indian texts not only dispels our doubts about the equal status of man and woman but also draws a roadmap for constructing an Indian Theory of Feminism. Some of the cardinal features of Indian feminism can be enumerated as (a) it opposes the monolithic and singular portrayal of Indian women, reductive understanding of multiple realities of Indian women, and supports to undifferentiated patriarchy; (b) it is critical of both homogenizing universalism and homogenizing differentials; (c) it opposes any value hierarchy such as a man being referred to in terms of culture, mind and reason and woman being referred to in terms of nature, body, and emotion; (d) it believes that a theory of feminism should be based on understanding rather than on justification, verification, and control; (e) it believes in a methodology which tries to analyze every fact-based on three parameters: (i) what is the status of the speaker? (ii) In whose name is the argument from the culture advanced? (iii) What is the degree of participation in the cultural formation of the social groups primarily affected by the artistic practice in question? (f) It is not proper to treat every woman as synonymous with a white woman. The lived experiences of women in different cultures shape their consciousness so that their worldview differs from those who have a degree of privilege.

Works Cited

Aristotle. *Generation of Animals*. Loeb Classical Library, 1943. Print.
Aristotle. *Politics I*. Oxford University Press, 1946. Print.
Aristotle. *The Art of Rhetoric*. Loeb Classical Library, 1967. Print.
De Beauvoir, Simone. *The Second Sex*. Penguin, 1949. Print.
Enloe, C. *Bananas Beaches and Base: Making Feminist Sense of International Politics*. University of California Press, 1989. Print.
Gadon, Elinor W. *The Once and Future Goddess*. Harper Collins, 1989. Print.

Hegel, Georg W. F. *Philosophy of Right*. Oxford University Press, 1973. Print.

Kane, Pandurang Vaman. *History of Dharmaśāstra*. Bhandarkar Oriental Institute, 1968. Print.

Klostermaier, Klaus. "Sri Tattva (The Goddess Principle)." *Journal of Vaisnava Studies* 4 (1995-96): 21-36. Print.

Manu. *Manusmriti*. Sri Thakur Prasad Pustak Bhandar, 1975. Print.

Minh-ha, Trinh T. *Woman, Native, Other: Writing Post Coloniality and Feminism*. Indiana University Press, 1989. Print.

Mohanty, Chandra Talpade. "Under Western Eyes: Feminist Scholarship and Colonial Discourses." *Boundary 2* 12.3 (1984): 333-358. Print.

Plato. *The Laws*. Leob Classical Library, 1968. Print.

Ṛg *Veda Samhita*. VADIKA Sanshodhan Mandala, 1946, Print.

Rousseau, Jean-Jacques. *Emile*, or *Treatise on Education*. E. P. Dutton, 1911. Print.

Sen, Gita and Caren Grown. *Development, Crises, and Alternative Visions: Third World Women's Perspectives*. Monthly Review Press, 1987. Print.

Spivak, Gayatri C. *In Other Worlds: Essays in Cultural Politics*. Routledge, 1988. Print.

Chapter 7

The Reconstruction of the Myth of Hindutva and the Great Indian Patriarchy

Guni Vats
Research Scholar,
Department of English,
University of Lucknow

Abstract

Myth has the power to weave a diverse society in a homogenous nation state, and indeed it is the only promise of a future that holds it all together. The postcolonial nation state called India has not only believed in but lived in myth, and the political scenario of the nation today is nothing short of the *manthan*. India, under the leadership of the masculine heroes of wide chests in its attempt to create the utopia of a *Hindutva* nation, is conveniently reinforcing the constructions of patriarchy. From *Bharat Maa* to *Gau Mata* to reliving the histories and myths of the great Indian wives, a careful reconstruction of Brahmanical patriarchy is underway and is conveniently consumed by the citizens hoping for a past they have never lived. My chapter attempts to read today's Indian political scenario as a text to study how myths have been exploited to construct a new Indian patriarchy; when every intellectual is busy saving the constitution, women take a back seat again.

Keywords: Myth, homogenous, postcolonial, patriarchy, democracy, manipulate.

* * *

Introduction

At the Calcutta Congress in 1917, Sarojini Naidu spoke about how women of India could sustain the nationalist movement, addressing any fears in the minds of their masculine counterparts. Twentieth-century India was agitating against foreign rule, and women played a significant role in igniting nationalism. India, a British colony, while attempting to break free from colonial rule, was also in the process of realizing itself as a nation. India was patriarchal, ruled by patriarchy, and in its chaos of becoming a Nation, its essence always stayed patriarchal. Women had to navigate through the patriarchal heads of the family and the government to even mark their existence in the struggle of becoming independent. From prostitution to child marriages to *sati* to *Bharatmata*, the women leaders had to dodge the expected constructions of their gender. The Indian woman was constructed as a simulation of the Indian mother, the developing struggles, and women groups were dedicated to producing better mothers who could make stronger sons for *Bharatmata*. Hindu mythology supplied the patriarchal ideologies with relevant examples from the *Puranas* and *Manusmriti*, exemplifying the goddesses who would be summoned when the gods were in distress. Once the threat was neutered, they were asked to return to their benevolent mother selves. The call for independence was a deafening frenzy, and the amalgamation of Hinduism with Nationalism stirred the plot a lot more. The nationalist Hindu identity became a rigid ideology, with its ideals of protecting Hindu women and thus hiding them in the boundaries of the home where any foreign influence would not corrupt them.

Twenty-first century India is an independent nation-state, but the roots of nationalist frenzy and patriarchy dig deep in its consciousness. The fight for independence did win the nation its freedom but left it with wounds that were hard to heal. The struggle had othered any foreign identity that the Hindu male would not identify with. Women were included in the peripheries of the existence of a self but restricted to the margins. The clever strategies of the British to divide and rule the sub-continent successfully created an ugly cleavage between Hindus and Muslims. The othering of the British was then displaced with the Muslims, and they became the other to the self of the Indian Hindu male. Ruling lords viewed India as a barbaric nation where the uncivilized men could not rule themselves, women as the vulgar displayers of their bodies, and festivals as obscene displays of erotic desires. Radha Kumar argues that "the internalization of Victorian morality grew so deep that almost any kind of public display of emotion began to be frowned upon, especially if it was physical" (36).

Indian conscience soon suffocated under Victorian morality and the social interaction changed to satisfy the colonial masters. "Holi celebrations could of course be fairly easily characterized as Bacchanalian or orgiastic, and it is not surprising that at the seventh National Social Conference reformers decided to launch a campaign to purify the Holi festivals so that people would neither drink, nor take drugs, nor dance during it" (Kumar 36). The Victorian standards of emotional restrictions were met to such extent that public mourning of Indian women, where they would beat their breasts and cry out loud, was restricted. In Punjab, *Siapa* (public mourning by women) was campaigned against by the seventh National Social reformers, disdaining such uninhibited emotion in public.

After seven decades of independence, the call for a New India is still finding itself echoed in the entanglements of nationalism, patriarchy, and Hindutva.

The colonial gaze seems to have taken a microscopical view in the age of globalization, where every act from political to private is sanitized off any traces of barbarianism left in its existence. The world has swiftly shifted towards the right, and India has followed suit. The Orientals have lived a long time under the scrutiny of the Occident, and now was time for India to reclaim its past without any hesitation of pacifying a Victorian overlord. But the construction of a tomorrow that is unapologetically walking with a history hand-in-hand has forced the constructed identities towards chaos. The Indian patriarch has guided the construction of its woman in the direction that the nation wants to achieve as a whole. The marginal parts of the country are left in chaos. An independent India was born from the womb of the Indian motherhood; the new India attempts to confine its women in the womb again. The roles of women in the nationalist struggle were limited to its feminine peripheries; the battle to become a New India aims to paint its women in the shadow of goddesses, to convey the greatness of the *Hindu Rashtra* (A Hindu nation). Women have always been a medium for man to achieve what he aims; she has always been a tool. In the saga of a new nation, she has transgressed her boundary carved out by the nationalist Hindu ideology and made India great again; she needs to respect her gendered boundaries. New India comes with new agents and new forms of dominance, but the essence of her patriarchy remains intact. In the narrative of Hindutva, she is pushed a little farther. At the same time, Hinduism allocated her a respected status. She, in Hindutva, is a passive site of construction, a Geist, an absence.

The Great Indian Patriarchy

Women and their rights have always been an agency of the men. A nation in chaos is expected to find stability in a *chora* (Plato calls *chora* the state of non-being), a maternal womb. Indian patriarchy is colored with a history of its colonization. The masculine identity in patriarchy relies on his role as a protector of the feminine; under foreign rule, stakes were higher. The Indian man struggled to become the man he thought he was. The idea of a man being a protector forced women into *zenanas* (inward section of home dedicated to women). The burden of freeing his nation and protecting his women traumatized Indian men so much that he was ready to accept regressive British laws until they promised to safeguard his women. The trauma of masculinity in being colonized was immense; the fear of castration became so real when his psyche was wounded every day with blames for him being effeminate. The Indian man was not like the British man; he was more expressive of his emotions and did not necessarily venture into arms and wars. He was an artist who understood and praised beauty without being vulgar; he was a performer who did not necessarily feel threatened to enact the roles of a woman. The colonizer's gaze bruised his identity and consciousness, and his immediate response was to punish the margins, for the center had shifted from his clutches. The Indian man was now on a mission to wash off any signs of effeminacy in his being; he hesitated from everything feminine, which further tensed the two genders' relationship. In his quest to become more of a man, he pushed his counterparts to behave like a proper woman. The great Indian patriarchy scarred its men and women; while both struggled to exist, men dominated to lay down the rules for a woman's existence. For the land of goddesses had limited its identity to the feminine icons of mothers and wives.

The acts of determining the places of women started with cleansing the lanes of prostitution. In the late nineteenth century, the social reform movements echo personal revolts like Ramabai's, and at that time, reform was centered on uplifting women and their political images. While the involvement of women was increasing and women delegation was allowed to enter the premises of national platforms, they were confined to delivering the vote of thanks to the President. When the discussions about women began in Congress, the first issue was prostitution. From 1889 to 1892, the Congress sessions presented and reiterated the need to abolish British laws regulating prostitution in India. The discussion was initiated after a British act, the Contagious Diseases Act, was passed post-1864. Radha Kumar recounts the brutal repercussions of the action, "many prostitutes committed suicide in despair at police harassment...on an average twelve women were arrested every day for breaches of the Act" (35). Indian leaders argued that the act had legalized prostitution indirectly rather than discouraging it. But, an inherent problem with the action was that the British "did not distinguish between prostitution and courtesanship, nor between the former and kept women, many of whom occupied places in respectable society" (35).

The act that brought all women under the umbrella of solicitation, even those who would earn by selling their art, constructed a new disdain for the work that was not cringed in ancient India. The contempt for prostitutes, courtesans, mistresses etched so deep in the Indian male psyche that men canceled any *nautch* performance at their homes. The discontent also created tension between the two genders, where labor was divided and stigmatized. The position of prostitutes, as a result, deteriorated; they did not hold the social situations they used to before the construction of the constructed norms of shame. Michael Madhusudan Datta was the first reformer to make any attempt at rehabilitating prostitutes in Calcutta. As a result, around ninety percent of Calcutta prostitutes were hired by the commercial theatres. Women would now play the roles scripted for them, which the men earlier played. Binodini, a prostitute from the same patriarchal disdain, shot to stardom through these theatres. Prostitutes were both English and native, but the inflated ego of the patriarchs never fought for their liberation. They were busy practicing racism at the expense of the other. From the frenzy of racism came the demands to protect their women from the other.

Constructing Indian Masculinity

Violence against women was prevalent, but with the deepening crevice of religion, the Masculine roles of a predator and a guardian were redefined. The atrocities afflicted by the self were ignored while the other was almost always colored as a Rapist. Indian men would now yell the "cries of protection of our women from sexual attacks by marauding white soldiers abounded, especially in Bengal" (Kumar 37). Rape was not only a violent attack against an individual but also a violation of a community's honor. Thus, women became the embodiment of their nation's honor and men their protectors. Rape was a taboo subject that was not to be discussed in public, only if a man of the same community commits it. If another committed rape, it was advertised and made a bone of contention. The death of Phulmoni Dasi in 1889 represents the othering of crime precisely. Attempts were made to hush the rape of a ten-year-old girl by her thirty-year-old husband, trying to consummate his marriage, because marital rape was legal and she met the criteria of the age of consent. The other registered a court case, and the Age of Consent Act was passed in 1891, which increased the age of consent to twelve. The othering of the perpetrator did not stop with the British; at the hint of communal divide, the other soon became the Muslim man, and the Indian woman would now have to be protected from him. A challenge that Indian Hindu patriarchs swear by even after years of independence and partition, as Radha Kumar would suggest: "Demands for Hindu self-defense groups began to be made, and the specter of the British soldier-rapist was now replaced by the specter of the Muslim rapist of Hindu women, leading to new calls for women to form their self-defense organizations" (41).

Indian masculinity was not a brainchild solely of the men; women had sewn together every inch of the masculine identity with precision. Women like Sarala Debi Ghoshal and Swarnakumari Debi are instrumental in constructing the Indian man in the nineteenth century colonized India. Sarala Debi was one of the "most militantly nationalist women of the period" (Kumar 40). In 1895, she became the editor of *Bharati*, a monthly journal in Calcutta, through which she would mobilize young men to "form *anantaranga dal* (intimate circle) for self-defense, and the defense of their women against British soldiers in streets and stations… she tied *rakhis* around their wrists as a token of their vow" (Kumar 39). In 1902, she organized pratapaditya *bratas* (fasts), where the young men were taught to wrestle and box and fight with weapons and swords. Pratapaditya was a Hindu landlord chosen by Sarala Debi. He elevated to the ranks of a warrior-hero to inspire the young men of her group to become a Hindu patriot like him. The following year she organized *udayatiya bratas* and *birastami bratas* (the ritualistic fasts to celebrate masculinity) that later took the form of a parade of physical prowess. While constructing masculine men, in an attempt to defy Macaulay's perception of Indian men as weak and cowardly, she opened an academy of martial arts, at which fencing would also be taught. She invented stories of great Indian kings and fighters to inspire her students to become heroic. While busy with her projects to create an army of strong men, she distinguished women's labor neatly. In 1910, she started Bharat Stree Mahamandal that educated women in things that suited them, "women should try and enrich the vernacular literature, organize selling centers for women's handicrafts and do what they could to afford medical treatment for women" (Kumar 39).

Post Bengal's partition, the cleavage between the Hindus and the Muslims became more apparent. Muslim League formed in Lahore in 1906, and soon after Sarala Debi and Ram Bhuj Datta founded Hindu Sahayak Sabha, the communal tensions pledged to protect their rights. The nation was now a mother, and the sons were Hindu; the aesthetic of nationalism mingles with the communal overdose bias to result in a highly masculine Hindu nationalist patriarchal nation-state. "In Bengal, goddess-centered nationalist rhetoric gained new ground as nationalism spawned revolutionary terrorism…anti-British feeling was imbued with a Hindu nationalism in which Kali was repeatedly invoked… Kali had been invoked to protect conservative Hindu tradition from Westernized reformers" (Kumar 44-45). Goddess Kali was evoked to protect Mother India's sons, "she became the liberator of Mother India, and a beacon for her nationalist sons" (Kumar 45). Kali, Durga, and Chandi are warrior goddesses in Hindu mythology. A representation from the margins; they are dark, fierce, unapologetic women who are not bound by the constraints of patriarchy. They were worshipped by dacoits and thieves and prostitutes and were forgotten for the most part. It was only through the process of a nationalist discourse of a Hindu identity that they had to be invoked. They were the representatives of femininity's fierceness and were worshiped to enjoy the frenzy of a Hindu nationalist becoming. Durga, the goddess of protection, and Kali, the goddess of devouring sexuality, were seen by intellectuals as the opposite poles of femininity. They would invoke the goddesses and post the fierce and violent battles; they would be requested to retreat. Durga Puja celebrates all faces of womanhood and immerses them in the ocean after they are prayed to. Women were invoked in the nationalistic struggle to fight the aggressive battle of independence, and were they then requested to retreat to their *zenanas*? As Radha Kumar suggests: "Despite these elements of the context in which Kali and Durga rose to dominance, or perhaps simultaneously defining and countering it, the new mother images also created new spaces for women...nationalist adoption of these images was crucial in creating these spaces" (45).

The strategy of invoking *Shakti* (the feminine strength) to the nationalist work also ensured that men could control their involvement in the entire process. Women were involved, but the Kali or Durga in them was never really allowed expression. They could form societies to spread awareness about hygiene, widow remarriages, education, maternity, and claim solidarity with the cause to the extent of presenting at speeches. Still, they were never really allowed to participate actively. The 1920s saw a greater enrolment in the nationalist struggle by women, but their roles were limited to protest passively; they were not allowed to get imprisoned or heckle with alcohol vendors. Even the relatives of prominent nationalist leaders had to suffice with a passive representation. The representation of the nation as a mother also served to marginalize the widows because they posed a threat to the patriarchy. Probably this is why *sati pratha* could not be done away with entirely, and strict rules were levied on Hindu widows. The widow was seen as the reason for her husband's death because she lacked in her ritual performances. She had to be contained before the epidemic would spread. Thus, the campaign to marry a widow as a sign of the service to the nation was encouraged because "widows as embodying a volatile and dangerously erotic energy...unchanneled to their husbands, was often expressed in the campaign for widow remarriage in the eighteen-fifties, and the campaign itself can be seen as attempting to re-channelize this energy by providing the widow with a husband" (Kumar 47).

The nation as *Bharat Mata*

Bande Mataram, initially written in 1875 as a page filler of the journal *Bangadarshan*, later became a part of Bankimchandra's novel *Anandamath* in 1882. Bankim Chandra Chatterjee had given a *mantra* to all the nationalist vigor. These verses beautifully realized the undercurrents of the patriarchal thirst. In 1896, Rabindranath Tagore sang it at the Calcutta session of the Indian National Congress. With Bankim came the realization that the idea of the nation was not an abstract piecing together of states but a homogenous consciousness that was the mother, the birth-giver, and the nurturer. Motherhood brought nostalgia, love, need, protection, nurturing, and all that *Manusmriti* had already taught the Hindus; how a mother was responsible for her sons. The realization of the nation as mother was not merely Bankim's verse or Tagore's music or Abanindranath's painting; it was now a personal relationship for every man who was a part of the nation; it was a war cry! The intellectuals made sure it remained so for when Bipin Chandra Pal wrote, "Our history is the sacred biography of the Mother. Our philosophies and the revelations of the Mother's mind...our religion is the organized expression of the soul of the Mother" (cited in Bose 1). He made sure that every action of the nation could be correlated with the physical existence of the mother. For Pal, the motherland was not how the West viewed it; it was "not a mere idea or fancy, but a distinct personality. The woman who bore them and nursed them, and brought them up with her own life and substance..." (cited in Bose 1). Once the nation successfully becomes a mother, the sons are obligated to save her dignity, preserve her soil and revere her existence. The construction of the nation as a mother thus cemented the patriarch son's complexes when he is answerable to the mother who has given birth to him and the *Bharatmata*.

Sara Suleri, in *The Rhetoric of English India*, explains how the "equation between a colonized landscape and the female body represents an alteritist fallacy" (230). She talks of a colonial gaze, which was not directed at the "inscrutability of an Eastern bride" (230) but rather to the "greater sexual ambivalence of the effeminate groom" (230). As a mother, the construction of the nation was not to construct the boundaries of women but a homoerotic site for the men to counter their effeminacy. Colonization did bind not only the geographical spaces but also constructed the psyche of the colonized. Ashish Nandy goes to lengths to explain how colonization was but a game of male anxiety and fantasy. Edward Said in *Orientalism* states how the colonizers had, through their paternalistic and condescending discourses, constructed Orient as the feminine, to be penetrated geographically, economically, and culturally. Irvin C. Schick's *The Erotic Margin* talks about how sexualizing geographical boundaries was central to the colonialist discourse of "narrative construction of spaces of otherness" (315). The discourse of colonial otherness and the construction of spaces were as binary as the Western understanding of gender, and thus, the boundaries that were penetrated were naturally rendered feminine. The construction of the colonized aversion towards femininity is also a post-colonial blotch the nation is trying to wash off. The masculinity had to be constructed in every male to throw the outsiders and prove that the Orient was not a mere effeminate tantalizing dream. The nation's construction as a mother was not to make it effeminate but kindle masculinity in the homoerotic masculine men of the country. The construction of the then masculine ideals has since been carried as the Orient has never shaken off the European gaze. It still measures its development on its yardsticks and thus promises to preserve its masculinity. The show of strength to the European world left us weak in our Eastern understanding of the genders and their construction; for now, myths had to be rewritten to accommodate the undying euphoria of masculinity. The Orient felt taunted at its effeminacy-constructed patriarchy that marginalized femininity as the weakness it never wanted to look back at.

The construction of a nation is not a mere political campaign. Geographical lines do no discern a nation. The nation has to be etched in the consciousness of its citizens, a national conscience that is reason enough for its citizens to sacrifice their lives. The construction thus involves the construction of psychology, and in a spiritual nation like India, mythologies needed to be constructed to empower the nationalizing mission. Exaggerated masculine narratives of mythological wars were created where the Gods played the role of a nationalist hero. For Indian women, Goddesses were as important as the macho protectors; they were the sympathizers, the *Shakti* of the revolution set at the margins to create a nation. Men looked up to the goddesses as their loyal devotees and invoked her to become their gentle mothers. Mrinal Pande in *Devi* (1996) writes, "since few Goddesses have children, in their secret wishes, men want to take their children's place and so reinvent the perfect mother, wild and fierce, yet loyal and all-pardoning" (xxi). The careful construction of the goddess myth is a testament to the nation's structure and the place of women in it. When required, she was conveniently seated at a pure and untouched pedestal by foreign forces; she became the virgin mother India never had. Even after nearly a century, India wakes to the idols of bejeweled mother clad in a red saree, all-forgiving, giver of wealth, of joy, of sons. India sleeps to the roaring songs of her devotion. These songs impress her, invoke the mother in her, and persuade her to give blessings while being the gullible, vulnerable idol of femininity. We have conveniently omitted the tales of Durga and Kali from the nation's conscience where she is a furious woman, untamed by the men who can govern the universe but cannot contain the femininity of the woman who has refused to abide by the laws of patriarchy. Pande states how we as a culture have been mute witnesses to this blind construction where all the corrupt, the rich, and the power mongers try to fill the gap with fake accounts designed to seem authentic. The saga of construction of Indian nationalism and the patriarchy accompanying is of creation without women; sons create their mothers, carefully painting every stroke of her existence.

Parashuram, a masculine Hindu epitome, a revered Vishnu incarnation, became an essential mythical character in the realization of a Hindu national male identity. The legend says that when all his elder brothers refused to murder their mother at their father's command, Ram obeyed without contradicting the patriarch leader. He beheaded his mother with a single fatal blow of the *Parashu* (ax). The sixth *avatar* of Vishnu thus became eternally etched in the psyche of the sons of *Bharatmata*, who swore to protect her but could do so only after they mutilated her. Partition of India shook the consciousness of the sons who wanted to preserve the mother's dignity. Still, mythology came to the rescue when Parashuram didn't only kill his mother but, at the mere chance of asking a boon, revived her to all her glory. The Indian son thus became Parashuram, the obedient son who would kill but also reinstate her. The myths, therefore, washed off the woman's role in creation when the patriarchs could decide the death and revival in a duty-bound discussion over boons and banes strictly corresponding to the hegemonic patriarchal structures of the home. The discourse aimed to empower men to fight for a nation that trapped its women in the fetters created to free the nation—the widely used emotive image in nationalist posters of *Srinkhalita Bharatmata* (the mother bound in chains). The process of being men pushed the others into the chaos of becoming women. This process involved literature that glorified the nation as a mother and constructed ideals of womanhood through mythical characters such as Sati, Savitri, Lilavati, Khana, and Arundhati. Women were indeed celebrated for their learning and wisdom, but who never once questioned their husbands, all the perfectly carved subjects of the patriarchal nation we were becoming.

The construction of a powerful nation required that the women were devoid of any human values. They were no more mere humans, they were either goddesses or whores, and they had to choose either of the extremes of construction. The marginalization of the other (the non-Hindus) did not stop at the other gender but also at the other religion. The sons of Mother India fought for her independence together, but in the struggle, they mutilated her for they could not unite on religious grounds. The signs of the rift were visible in the early stages for when the saffron-clad woman was made to be the mother; the color of her saree had already divided her sons on religious grounds. Since the very conception of *Bande Mataram*, Muslims were left alienated for the novel in which the national song was included was filled with anti-Muslim prejudices. The divide worsened with every clarification that followed, "suggesting that Bankim meant British when he said Muslim, simply added insult to injury" (Bose 15). The bigotry was not hard to be traced, but the sons who went to fight for the mother-nation saw no sense in othering the other religious community. Aurobindo believed that what Bankim Chandra Chatterjee was trying to propagate in the idea of an undivided India was an over-optimistic dream which would never be realized in reality, "the Bharatmata that we ritually worshipped in the Congress was artificially constructed, and she was the companion and favorite mistress of the British, not our mother…" (cited in Bose 22). His fear was not that India could never be united but that the undivided Indian image was a Hindu nation's image; Abanindranath's painting was that of a Hindu's mother, and for the complete realization of our nationhood, a new inclusive idea was required. Edward Said in *Culture and Imperialism* explains how "culture's contribution to statism is often the result of a separatist, even chauvinist and authoritarian conception of nationalism" (217). So, all the intellectual and cultural energy of the nation that has just risen from colonization must be directed towards reconceptualizing the society and culture, not prejudiced by old orthodoxies and injustices.

Hindutva

Where Congress was worried that a section of Indians was left out of the nationalist debate, another section, the Hindu leaders and intellectuals, ensured that Hindu as a creed was not left behind in constructing a secular tomorrow. The first edition of *Hindutva* by Vinayak Damodar Savarkar was released in 1923. The book promised to define the notion of Hindutva as the way of life that terminologies as Hinduism failed to do. The book determined to tie the Hindus in a homogenous identity, for the book "revealed to them their real National-self, in which and through which consciously or unconsciously they lived and moved and had their organic being" (Savarkar 9). Savarkar, through his book, constructed a self, for the process of othering was incomplete until a self was established as a solid organic homogenous identity. Scholars like Mahatma Gandhi have preached how Hinduism was an all-inclusive religion and never marginalized or rejected any individual or religious sect. Savarkar differed and recorded his dissent in the book that later became the founding stone for many that believed in India as a *Hindu-Rashtra*. He propagated the idea of Hindutva, stating that it was a terminology in totality, the amalgamation of the Hindu culture, history, nation and religion, Hindu people as a whole. India became synonymous with Hindus. He asserted that "India must stand or fall with the fortunes of the Hindus" (Savarkar 91). He did preach loyalty and devotion to the nation, but Hindu's commitment towards a Hindu nation. For him, India was no more the sacred mother but the "fatherland (*pitribhu*) and the holy land (*punyabhu*) of Hindus" (Savarkar 115).

With the emergence of Hindu nationalism, the hegemony was constructed parallelly, and the price was India's independence. To create a Hindu nation was required to inject the population with the elixir of an identity that was glorified for their lives to mean something even though the years of slavery had proved otherwise. Hinduism was a milder dose of the adrenaline required to pump the majority, and thus came the slogans of Hindutva that were well defined and a cult that had a leader to its right. "Hindutva is not a word but a history...a history in full," whereas "Hinduism is only a derivative, a fraction, a part of Hindutva" (Savarkar 3). The creation of self never rested to realize that the self could rule his land and did not need an overlord but vigorously created a non-self. Savarkar believed that the feeling of selfhood could not be evoked until the non-self was made and the conflict between the two celebrated. He writes in his book that "nothing can weld peoples into a nation and nations into a state as the pressure of a common foe" (Savarkar 43). The creation of a familiar foe, the non-self, the non-Hindu, is essential that the twenty-first century India is suffering from. When the veins of a nation are poisoned with othering, hatred rises from the dormant fanatic section whenever the identity of self is in danger. Savarkar is not a weak practitioner of Hinduism; he is a robust masculine patriarch, a man celebrated as *veer* today, and he is not afraid of hatred; he even endorses it. He explains how hate if baked well, acts as a unifier "Hatred separates as well as unites" (39). Savarkar celebrates the "bonds of common blood" (84) of Hindus, for he believes Hindus are not just citizens of the Indian state and are united in their motherly love to protect their land, but they are a race – *jati*.

The introduction of Savarkar's *Hindutva* in the nationalist debate created chaos, a *Manthan* (churning) that marginalized the non-Hindus and women. The depiction of *Bharatmata* might have contained the portrayal of women in narrow spheres. Still, the evocation of the nation as the fatherland and the holy land wiped her off the table completely. When patriarchs decided to celebrate their *jati* in the name of common brotherhood, it completely omitted any discussion about women. The only place that Savarkar gives to women in his book is when he talks of marriage and crossbreeding or advertising the purity of the innocent Hindu women who listen to the "cradle songs of Sita, the good" (Savarkar 93). He mentions Savitri and Damyanti as the ideals of purity as if issuing performance notices for the Hindu maid. He does talk of love but then compares it to Radha's love. He curates' examples from the mythological history where women were represented as the ideals of patriarchal values. If the essentials of Hindutva were to construct a nation, it is needless to say what the position of women might be, for they were not even involved actively in the construction of self. The nation born secular has undergone chaos after seven decades of its inception when the Hindutva nationalism has surfaced the fanatic spaces that were suppressed in the acts of secular progress. The intoxication that leaders like Savarkar had placed Hindu men in probably never left their minds, for they jumped at the next war cry of becoming a Hindutva nation and voted a party in the majority that promised to fulfill this dream. It was then needless to examine how the masculine epitome of the patriarchal national self was celebrated as the *karma yogi*. This lone man had sacrificed his family and given up his desires to work for the nation. The woman in the celebration of the *yogi* was reduced to a mere wish, an *apsara*, and a hindrance to the way forward.

The binarism of the inner and the outer

Detangling the strands of colonialism, a cultural and political space was extracted that was seen as contradictory. "Chatterjee's analytical binarism sharply separating the inner, spiritual from the outer, material domain" (Bose 27) was the exaggerated division of a nation that was trying to define itself, torn between the two domains. The Indian nation-state was gendered borrowing the gendering scheme of the colonizers, and women were conveniently locked in the inner spheres. After shaking off the chains of colonization, the nation-state refused to construct an alternative space and remained trapped in the nation, functioning as an extension of the family. The structures that should have represented women now became a vast space of their construction. Women in the making of the nation thus never seem to hold firm ground in the decision-making process, for they are always under the patriarchal gaze that extends from their home to the parliament. Ages have witnessed outsiders, in the form of missionaries and colonizers, trying to protect the Indian woman from the strictly sewn patriarchal structures of Vedic India. The outside gaze worsened the position of women as it not only restricted their mobility to the boundaries of the home and alerted the patriarch of the safety of his woman, and he restricted her further. It only pushed her behind purdah with every foreign attempt to free the Indian woman (a veil). To successfully create a new India, remember and celebrate the Vedic India, claiming a false homogeneity and a golden past. The revolutionaries that had taken it on them to construct a new nation redefined women's roles and brought her sexual freedom and character to the discourse of the public domain. The patriarch leaders of the house would openly settle a contract with other patriarchs on an unsaid promise of delivering the woman pure at the time of marriage. Maharshi Dayanand Saraswati in *Satyartha Prakash* explains how the girl and the boy behave at the time of their wedding discussions and how they must be virgins for creating a robust Arya Samaj. He conveys in detail how and when the "man and woman must have sex, how menstruation is impure and what must be done during and after pregnancy" (41). Once the spiritual leader, clad in saffron, declares his intentions for constructing a stronger nation and holds the baton for woman's education, whatever he says next is taken at face value.

The New Woman

Colonization was a civilizing mission for the Indian men, and once they achieved *Swaraj*, they were determined to civilize their women. National projects for women emancipation were employed, and tiny victories like the abolition of *sati* in 1829 and widow remarriage in 1856 were achieved. The new woman was seen as the female counterpart of the new male elite who would share the sensibilities of the men in the family. She was burdened with freeing herself of the world's understandings and protecting and traditionally looking after her home. Sumit Sarkar, a Renaissance reformist, blames Rammohan and Vidyasagar not to be full-blooded liberals because they never worked for the complete emancipation of Indian women. They did fight for the woman not to be burnt at her husband's pyre but never did fight the hypocritic ideals of patriarchy or even the injustices in the caste structures. Kumari Jayawardena calls the acts of emancipation selective as it was confined only to the upper castes, she says that the revolutionary process of liberation was limited to *Sati* and widow remarriage because "they could safely be tackled because they had not existed in very early times, confined to upper castes and classes and, if remedied, would have given India the appearance of being civilized without endangering the traditional family structures" (Jayawardena 80). Lata Mani questioned the reformists for how did their reforms forget the very subjects they were reforming. She points out how women were absent from any discussion about them, men discoursed about the act of *sati* in a gathering full of men, where men would decide, and men would contest, none thought of asking a widow if she wanted to sit on the pyre or not. In the discussions of redefining Indianness and tradition, the Vedic tradition was at stake and not women; she had to be reformed under the guidelines laid by the men.

If India was gendered in the nineteenth century, the twentieth century was deciphering where the European hands had touched their *Bharatmata* and how she was corrupted. The only domain Indian man could look at without the embarrassment of failing to protect the honor of their women; their existence was the home. The traditional domestic space that was the woman's domain was the only Indian space left, and the men determined to keep it so. In his essay "The Nationalist Resolution of the Women's Question" (1989), Partha Chatterjee studies how Indian women were caught between the pressures of colonial modernity and traditional national sentiments. The overeducated women would be tagged as the memsahibs ignoring her children and her husband, and the illiterate woman was the man's failure to civilize his home. "Give no place in your heart to memsahib-like behavior. This is not becoming a Bengali housewife. See how an educated woman can do housework thoughtfully and systematically in a way unknown to an ignorant, uneducated woman" (Chatterjee 325). Her understanding of the world would thus be tested only when applied to the home, much like the Victorian housewife. This world, the image of a nation was once again linked with the image of an Indian woman, who is a chaste wife and a mother, a pure sister and a good woman, and who promises to build the home and the world together, without sacrificing her intellects or her tradition. In the second decade of the twenty-first-century version of a new India, she again goes missing from the discourse, reduced to being the site of agendas, the beneficiary of schemes but not an active citizen. She is torn between the Hindutva world and the home she has nurtured for so long. The New Woman will have to rise from the ashes of the many who sacrificed themselves for the woman today to launch satellites to Mars and represent the defense forces in the Republic Day parade.

The twenty-first-century world eagerly tilts towards the right, promises purity of creed, freedom from refugees, and abandonment of all liberal, pseudo-intellectual thoughts. Following the world's way, India shifted towards the right-wing ideologies and unveiled its dark corners filled with bigotry and hatred.

The influence of right-wing ideologies worldwide is not limited to their heavy-handedness over liberal values and their attempts to celebrate the hyper-masculinity of the typical patriarchal societies where women are doubly marginalized. The Lok Sabha of 2019 enjoyed maximum representation of women members of the parliament, but the discussion of sensitive bills like the Protection of Transgender Rights Bill or the Citizenship Amendment Bill fell on deaf ears. Even in the parliamentary debate relating to rapes, an honorable member of the parliament demanded the culprits be lynched. Right-wing politics give birth to right-wing patriarchy beyond the centuries of progress and quotes from ancient scriptures. They hail Gods from political stages and expect women to take up their space at the corner of the discourse. Women's role has to be tailored to match the Hindu nationalist ideology in a nation that is in the making of becoming a *Hindu Rashtra*.

To normalize the Hindu ideals come examples of women like Jijabai, the mother of Shivaji, a woman of virtue, the mother of the dream of *swaraj* (self-rule). This holy womb produced a son like the great Maratha warrior. Women were thus carefully constructed to hail motherhood and detest foreign influences. For nearly four centuries after Jijabai's existence, the cinema screens revere her son and Tanhaji, another great warrior. The Muslims, through these movies, are portrayed as monotone carnivores. The conscience of Hindus is aptly fed with the foe, the Muslim invaders who had once broken into the houses of Hindus and abducted their women, killed their sons, and owned their lands. Women in all this construction become the object for which wars were launched. Today, the Hindu woman is reborn as the vulnerable object every time such movies hit the screen or media reminds the public of the Hindu Muslim debate at prime time. The history is rewritten with every construction of the Hindu ideology. With every phoneme of the new history, women get trapped in the bondage of being the damsels a little more. When *Sadhvis* (nuns) as elected representatives come to the fore, they only reiterate the phobia of the other a little more, for the saffron-clad woman is the ideal Hindu mother. She is asexual and devoted to the cause of the caste and the nation. She satisfies the colonial appetite of the virgin mother, the purity of the home.

Violence against women

Benedict Anderson in *The Imagined Community* states nation to not be a physical homogenous, geographically defined structure but an "imagined community" (54). For him, the nation is, however, the citizen imagines it to be, and thus, the relations in the imagined community are also envisioned. The role of women in the imagined structure is not how women imagine it to be but how the men have imagined their positions to be. Woman in the process of nationalism becomes her feminine self. Reading the East-West dichotomy, the West had imagined the Eastern woman as the sensual, erotic subject. The woman painted in the caves of Ajanta or the woman sculpted on the walls of Konark. The Hindu man thus busied himself with the project to wash off his woman of the western gaze of her sensuousness and kept her protected behind a veil. Woman today is still behind the veil, peeping from behind but still behind it. The twenty-first century educated man fights with the orthodox man, the traditional self-fighting with the modern self to decide how to accommodate the feminine. The discourses have happened; the media has used the term feminism on a loop so much that it has tired its audience. Feminism has become synonymous with women and a vice associated with any woman who learns to speak for herself. Nirbhaya rape case in 2012 brought the youth to the streets; men and women were both fighting for justice for a woman who was punished for being out on the streets with a male friend in the late hours. The act of woman had taunted the freedom of the patriarch who was taught to keep his woman in etiquette, and he knew only one language to overcome the shame the liberty of women subjected to him. His act was the only reaction he was taught. They, in their minds, were still the Parashuram who had to mutilate the mother to reinstate *dharma* (religion).

Sexual violence as a lesson does not end with Nirbhaya, but the protest to have a voice in the public space begins from her. In a nation declared by international agencies as unsafe for women, rapes aren't uncommon. Indian media deals with the horrific cases, normalize the act, and serve it at the drawing-room debates. The protests died down and with the issues of Kathua and Unnao, the heat simmered. Screen time of such gruesome acts reduced, and so did the audience's patience that was subjected to watch the cruelty. Rapes served both purposes, and the intellectuals came on the street to demand justice, and the boundaries of the home shrink a few more inches. Newspapers and defenders of the public discipline advocated for the woman to equip herself whenever she steps out, wear decent clothes, behave un-sensuously, and use her sixth sense to sniff the molester.

Advisories for the victim further pushed them to victimhood and reduced their involvement in the public space. The Hyderabad rape case of the 27-year-old doctor shook the nation once again. Still, the drama of the vengeance of the police further pushed the nation-state into the chaos that only celebrated patriarchy. Since the very inception of patriarchy, men have been symbolized as the messiah. From cinema to literature to mythology, man is the ultimate protector of the woman and her dignity. So, when the police shot down the alleged culprits, they were welcomed with petals, how Shri Ram was welcomed back to Ayodhya. The man had reinstated *Dharma* by protecting the woman once again. Putting legalities aside, when a man decides to act as a woman's protector, he alone holds the right to violate her dignity. He then is the hero and the villain in the movie where she is but the love interest. When the film is played in real life, it becomes scary because it then constructs a patriarchal regime of a democratic country that will be difficult to shake off.

Conclusion

Myths are but a biased cultural construction. The semiology of myth dictates a specific meaning that is more often than not colored with the bias of hierarchy. The reading and interpretation of these myths complete the circle of the meaning-making process. Human beings are symbol-using animals; they understand and perceive the world only through the symbols surrounding them. The symbols are already loaded with hierarchical explanations. The process of deciphering their meanings also clung to the structure responsible for constructing them; hence, the circle of the order of hierarchy becomes complete. Myths try to project perfection in the world. Once dominant meaning has been established, even before they are surrendered to the process of signification, that meaning shows itself as the truth. It forms a society with a mythic idea of perfection and truth. If myths are mere emplotments, then the fable and plot need a hero to understand and perceive right. The narrator, the savior, the protector, the creator, the destroyer on whom is dependent a perfect tomorrow that society of today strives for and myths promise. Heroes are perfectly created characters of the fables of a myth that ensure myth-making to be a process that reaches its intended conclusion. They are the pioneers of the hierarchy of the organization. They are the masculine epitome of the upper-class idea of what perfection must be. They are, and the rest is in-relation-to-them. They are the being; the rest is becoming. They are the self, all rest is the other, and this other is defined concerning them. Most of the time, in the process of the myth-making only hero, get an established and detailed construction; his demeanor, his clothes, his fantasies, his stories, his protégé is all minutely constructed while his other, the heroine, is left at the altar to be understood as whatever he is not.

Heroes not only define women but, in most cases, construct them. They assume roles that, in turn, define the boundaries or the character of the heroines. When Ganesha is created as the doorkeeper to safeguard his mother, who would ultimately fight his father to protect his mother, Parvati is pushed inside the threshold of the household not only by her husband but also by her son, a neat transition of the role of protector from the father to the son. Hindu mythology is a cyclical paradigm where the idea of hero changes with every shift in time; from Brahma of *Upanishads* to Purusha of *yoga* to Shiva of *tantra*, from Rama to Krishna, the values change, and so does the definition of masculinity. The changing face could also be understood by reading Vishnu's incarnations chronologically; Parashurama, who killed his mother, was the Hindutva hero, Rama saving the damsel and slaying the enemy and then proving wife's purity is the *Purushottam*, Krishna celebrating love and wit is a God who is the most human-like, Balarama reducing Revati to the proper size to marry her constructing the ideals of marriageable girls, Chaitanya, the god for immoral women. Hanuman, the masculine epitome of a son, was his father's compensation to his wife for impregnating her. This act seems to have taken place without her consent but the promise of a god-like son forgiving the patriarch of the front of forced copulation. The hero has always been Plato's philosopher carrying men to the light at the end of the tunnel, but the heroines in these constructions are often left in the dark.

The hero myths in Hindu mythology are many. Still, the reconstruction of the myth of Hindutva and Indian patriarchy must be analyzed to realize if we are still stuck in the myth-making. Kristeva analyses the mother-son relationship a lot different than what the chapter has discussed, she realizes that "the mother becomes the object of the infant's concerns...she is not an object as distinct from himself but in connection to himself, as its first *imago*, meaning a phantasm – an object the subject reacts to as if it were real" (Kristeva 33). The mother is not another for the son, and she is the phallic signifier. *Bharatmata*, for a Hindu son, is his self; it is because of her that he signifies the world. She is never the referent but the concept. She is the reminiscence that he desires; he desired to be independent. Seen psychoanalytically, the relationship of a Hindu son with his nation-mother appears much more apparent and explains how he then defines women's role in it. Women nationalist militants themselves constructed space from them, from which the twenty-first-century woman is trying to break free. The fight for her identity is endless, and the construction of biased meanings never leaves her existence, but she fights to be who she is amidst the myth of Hindutva and the great Indian patriarchy.

Works Cited

Anderson, Benedict. *Imagined Communities: Reflections on the Origin and Spread of Nationalism*. Verso, 1983. Print.

Bose, Sugata. *The Nation as Mother*. Penguin, 2017. Print.

Chatterjee, Partha. "The Nationalist Resolution of the Women's Question." *Recasting Women: Essays in Colonial History*. Ed. Kumkum Sangari and Sudesh Vaid. Zubaan, 1989. 35-114. Print.

Jayawardena, Kumari. *Feminism and Nationalism in the Third World*. Verso, 2016. Print.

Kristeva, Julia. *Powers of Horror: An Essay of Abjection*. Columbia University Press, 1980. Print.

Kumar, Radha. *The History of Doing: An Illustrated Account of Movements for Women's Rights and Feminism in India, 1800-1990*. Zubaan, 1993. Print.

Pande, Mrinal. *Devi: Tales of the Goddess in Our Time.* Penguin, 1996. Print.
Said Edward. *Culture and Imperialism.* Vintage Books, 2014. Print.
Saraswati, Maharshi Dayanand. *Satyarthprakash.* Mata Tulsadevi, 2018. Print.
Savarkar, Vinayak Damodar. *Hindutva.* Veer Savarkar Prakashan, 1969. Print.
Schick, Irvin C. *The Erotic Margin: Sexuality and Spatiality in Alteritist Discourse,* Verso, 1999. Print.
Suleri, Sara. *The Rhetoric of English India.* University of Chicago, 1992. Print.

Contributors

Diana J. Fox is Professor of Anthropology, Department Chair, and founding editor of the *Journal of International Women's Studies* at Bridgewater State University. Her feminist decolonial scholar-activism is predicated on partnerships with social movement actors in Jamaica, Trinidad & Tobago, Nepal, Sri Lanka, and Japan working on gender and sexual diversity issues, women's social movement activism for ecological sustainability, women's human rights, and transnational feminisms.

Waseem Anwar is Professor (English) and Director (ICPWE) at Kinnaird College, Lahore. He worked at Forman Christian College and Government College universities as Dean (Humanities) and Chair (English). A Fulbright scholar (twice), former President of the PUAN and Fulbright Alumni Association, he is the recipient of *Gale Group American Scholar*, "Salam Teacher Award – 2004" and HEC "Best Teacher Award – 2003." He is serving the SALA Executive Committee for 3rd time, and his academic credits include *"Black" Women's Dramatic Discourse, South Asian Review* (31:3), and a range of articles and conferences.

Diptarup Ghosh Dastidar is a research scholar working on Indian comics from Banaras Hindu University (BHU). His other areas of interest range from music, manga, and world comics to video games and tabletop games (deckbuilding and role-playing mostly), and he has publications in the domain of Indian comics and graphic medicine in reputed journals published by Johns Hopkins University Press and Routledge Taylor & Francis among others. Mr. Ghosh Dastidar is currently also an Assistant Professor in Amity School of Languages, Amity University, Chhattisgarh.

Chand Basha M is an Assistant Professor, Research Guide, and Chairperson for the Board of Examination of Dept. of English at Vijayanagara Sri Krishnadevaraya University, Ballari, Karnataka (India). He is also a Research Associate at the Shia'ah Institute, London, United Kingdom. His areas of interest include decolonial thought, contemporary literature, and sites of memory. He has presented research papers at the University of Leeds, School of Oriental and African Studies, the Shia'ah Institute (England), the University of Muenster, the University of Augsburg (Germany), the University of Utrecht (the Netherlands), etc.

Abhisek Ghosal is currently working as a senior Ph.D. Research scholar at the Department of Humanities and Social Sciences in Indian Institute of Technology, Kharagpur, India. He holds M.A. and M.Phil. degrees to his credit. His broad areas of research interest are Critical Theory, Continental Philosophy, South Asian Literature, Criminology, and Globalization Studies. He has published articles in different leading academic journals, either SCOPUS indexed or UGC approved, in the world.

Feroza Jussawalla is Professor Emerita of English at the University of New Mexico in Albuquerque. Her most recent co-edited book is *Memory, Voice and Identity: Muslim Women's Writing from Across the Middle East* (Routledge, 2021). She is also co-editor of *Emerging South Asian Women's Writing* (Peter Lang, 2017) and *Interviews with Writers of the Postcolonial World* (Mississippi, 1997), editor of *Conversations with V.S. Naipaul* (Mississippi, 1999), and author of *Family Quarrels: Towards a Criticism of Indian Writing in English* (Peter Lang, 1984). Her collection of poetry is entitled *Chiffon Saris*.

Adam Short is a mathematics student, soccer coach, writer, and father living in Richmond, Virginia. After being surprised to learn of the role of Black filmmakers in the early history of the film while he was researching an adaptation project, he resolved to do his part to advance the modern understanding of the essential contributions of black and indigenous people to the development of American culture.

Chandrakala Padia retired as senior-most professor of the university from the Department of Political Science, Banaras Hindu University, Varanasi, India. She served the university in different capacities: Head, Department of Political Science, Dean, Faculty of Social Sciences; Director, Centre for Women's Studies and Development, B.H.U., and Director, Centre for Integrated Rural Development. She also served as Chairperson, UGC Standing Committee on Women's Studies, Vice-Chancellor, MGS University, Bikaner, Rajasthan, and Chairperson, Indian Institute of Advanced Study, Rashtrapati Nivas, Shimla. Her academic credit includes twelve national and international awards and fellowships; nearly fourteen authored and edited books; and more than seventy research articles published in the journals and magazines of scholarly repute.

Guni Vats is a Research Scholar at the University of Lucknow. An avid researcher and a passionate feminist, she has been published in more than twenty books. Writing since an early age, she has developed a keen interest in Gender Studies and Indian Mythology. She has extensively researched the nuances of patriarchy and is trying to deconstruct Indian Femininity. She is a curious soul and aims to shift the center, one question at a time.

Index

A

Abolitionism 72
ambivalence viii, xxii, 35, 104
anti-Muslim 40, 44, 106
antebellum 69, 71, 79
Ardhanarishwar 93, 94
artifacts xxiv, 20, 21, 22, 23, 24, 26, 28, 29, 30, 31
Ayad Akhtar viii, 35, 36, 42, 46

B

Bande Mataram 103, 106
Ben Ali 66, 67, 68, 74, 76, 77, 78
Bharatmata 98, 104, 105, 106, 108, 110, 114
bigotry 106, 110
black history ix, 65
black liberation ix, 65
Black Lives Matter xii, 52, 53, 54, 55
Blackness xiv, 68, 70
border thinking 15

C

capital 3, 4, 15, 19, 37
capitalism xxiv, 6, 49
Capitulation vi, vii
Chicano 47, 53, 54, 55
Chora 99
Citizenship Amendment Bill 111
civilize v, vi, 68, 69, 70, 71, 72, 73, 83, 93, 98, 109, 110
colonialism v, vi, vii, viii, xii, xiii, xiv, xviii, xix, xx, xxii, xxiii, 4, 5, 6, 49, 50, 52, 53, 54, 55, 108

coloniality xviii, 3, 4, 5, 6, 7, 8, 10, 12, 14, 15, 16, 17, 52, 56, 59
colonization vii, xviii, 4, 47, 50, 52, 59, 83, 99, 104, 106, 108, 109
Countermyth 72
cultural amnesia x, 35, 36, 40, 41, 44, 45, 46
cultural fetishism 24, 27

D

decolonial xviii, xxi, xxii, xxiii, xxiv, 3, 4, 5, 7, 9, 10, 11, 12, 15, 19, 20, 22, 28, 29, 31, 32, 47, 49, 50, 51, 52, 54, 58, 59, 60, 61, 66
decolonization xvii, xviii, xix, xx, xxi, xxii, xxiii, xxiv, xxv, 29, 48, 51, 52, 53
de-colonialism xviii
decoloniality vii, viii, xi, xii, xiv, 4, 5, 6, 15, 17, 19, 21, 28, 29, 30, 31, 32, 47, 48, 50, 52, 58, 61, 65
democratization xvii, xviii, xxi, xxiii
development vii, xi, xxiv, 3, 11, 13, 15, 48, 83, 90, 92, 95, 104
dharma 92, 112
diaspora 66, 67, 75, 76
Disgraced x, 35, 36, 42, 45, 46
Dualism 91

E

East-West 112
Edward Said xii, xx, xxv, 48, 49, 104, 106, 115
epistemological iii, xiv, xxv, 28, 30, 31, 32, 82

epistemologically 19
epistemic endosmosis 40, 41, 43
epistemic violence xii
erotic 112
Eurocentric ix, xxi, xxiii, 3, 4, 6, 27, 31, 81, 82, 87, 93
exhibition 26, 31, 33

F

feminist ix, xiii, xiv, xv, xxii, 81, 82, 83, 84, 86, 91, 93, 94, 95
feminism vii, ix, xiv, xv, 81, 82, 85, 87, 91, 92, 93, 94, 95, 112, 114
Frantz Fanon xx, xii, xxiv, 16, 61
Fulani 70, 71

G

Geechee/Gullah 66, 67, 73, 74, 75, 76, 77
geopolitics xxi
globalectical reading 29
graphic viii, xxiii, 3, 4, 6, 7, 11, 14, 15, 16,

H

hegemonic xvii, xx, xxi, 6, 16, 40, 50, 106
Hindu Rashtra 99, 111
Hindutva vii, ix, xiii, xxiii, 97, 98, 99, 107, 108, 110, 114, 115
history v, vi, vii, viii, ix, xi, xii, xiii, xix, xxii, xxiii, xiv, 4, 6,7, 20, 21, 22, 25, 27, 29, 30, 31, 48, 49, 50, 52, 55, 61, 65, 66, 68, 75, 76, 79, 80, 95, 99, 103, 107, 108, 111, 114
historiography 24, 26, 29
homogenous 97, 103, 107, 111
human regression xi, 3
humility xi, xiv, xv

I

ideology v, xi, xii, xiii, xxiii, 3, 28, 98, 99, 110, 111
ideological xiii, xix, xx, 28, 29, 31, 72
imagined xviii, xx, 12, 24, 26, 27, 29, 30, 111, 112, 114
immigrants viii, 38, 44, 45, 46, 57
imperial v, vi, xii, xvii, xix, xx, 5, 6, 7, 9, 21, 22, 24, 28, 29, 30, 31, 32, 48, 106, 115
Indian theory of feminism ix, 81, 82, 85, 93, 94
indigeneity vi, xx
intellectual ix, xi, xi, xiv, xv, xxi, xxiii, 31, 79, 85, 90, 97, 102, 106, 107, 110, 112
Islamic 29, 33, 35, 36, 38, 39, 41, 42, 43, 44, 45, 46, 65, 66, 67, 75, 78, 80
Islamophobia viii, xiii, xxi, 35, 36, 38, 39, 39, 40, 43, 44, 45, 46
Istanbul 19, 20, 21, 23, 25, 27, 31

J

Jauhar 56, 57
Jenny Colon bag 25, 27

L

La Llorona viii, 47, 52, 53, 54, 55, 56, 57, 58, 59, 60, 61

M

Malinche 52, 53, 54, 55, 56, 57, 60
marginalization 36, 106
Manusmriti 85, 92, 95, 98, 103
masculinist 91, 94
masters v, vi, vii, 98
matriarch 50, 76

Meditations xiv, 66, 67, 73, 76, 77, 78, 79
memory viii, xxiii, 3, 4, 12, 19, 20, 22, 24, 28, 30, 40, 41, 46, 75, 78
memsahib 110
methodology xii, xiv, 87, 93, 94
minority 40, 52, 53, 54
Muhammad, Bilali ix, xiv, 65, 66, 68, 71, 72, 76, 77, 78, 79
myth v, vi, vii, viii, xi, xiii, xxii, xxiii, xxiv, 3,4,8,11,12, 16, 47, 48, 49, 50, 51, 52, 53, 54, 55, 56, 57, 59, 60, 61, 68, 76, 97, 104, 105, 113, 114

N

nationalism xiii, xx, 22, 58, 59, 97, 98, 102, 105, 106, 107, 108, 112, 114
nationalist xiii, xx, 52, 60, 97, 98, 99, 101, 102, 103, 105, 106, 107, 108, 110, 111, 114
New Woman 109, 110
New India 98, 99, 109, 110
Nirbhaya 112

O

orientalism xx, 22, 35, 40, 41, 46, 48, 61, 104
orgullo 54

P

Papal Bull vi
Pamuk, Orhan viii, 19, 20, 30, 31, 32, 33
parampara ix, 82, 92
patriarchal xi, xiii, 80, 84, 97, 98, 100, 102, 103,

patriarchy vii, ix, xiii, xv, xxiii, 83, 93, 94, 97, 98, 99, 100, 102, 103, 104, 105, 109, 111, 112, 114, 118
post-9/11 viii, xxii, 35, 36, 37, 39, 40, 41, 43, 46
postcolonial v, vii, viii, ix, x, xi, xii, xvii, xviii, xix, xx, xxi, xxii, xxiii, 6, 21, 28, 32, 35, 36, 39, 40, 46, 48, 49, 50, 56, 58, 61, 97106, 108, 109, 111, 113
postcolonialism vii, xi, xviii, xxiv, xxv, 4, 48, 50, 58
postcoloniality xvii, xxiv, 48
postmodern 6, 31
Prakriti/Purush 86
pre-colonial xii, xiii, xix
precolonialism xviii
purushottam 114

Q

Quetzalcoatl 47, 55, 60
Qu'ran 65, 66, 80

R

rape 57, 72, 101, 111, 112
rationality 4, 16, 82, 91, 92, 94
raza 53, 54,
regression vii, xi, xviii, 3, 4, 9, 15
renaissance xix, xxi, 4, 45, 110
resonance 25, 26, 33
Rg Veda Samhita 84,85, 86, 87, 95
River of Stories vii, viii, xi, 3, 4, 6, 7, 10, 12, 13, 14, 15, 17

S

Sahadharmini 93, 94
Sen, Orijit vii, viii, 3, 4, 6, 10, 13, 14
self-awareness xi, 60
self-fighting 112

Siapa 98
socio-political 19, 83
spatio-temporal ix, 23, 25, 26
surveillance xxii, 35, 45
swaraj 109, 111

T

Tale of Things viii, 19
Tashif 66
Terra Nullius vi
The Museum of Innocence viii, 19,
  20, 22, 27, 28, 30, 31, 33
Third World Women 83, 84, 95
Thiong'o, Ngugi wa xxi, xxiv, xxv, 4,
  9, 12, 21, 29, 33, 49
transnational viii, 35, 36
Transgender Rights Bill 111
Twin Towers 35, 36, 37

U

umma 67

V

Vedic 84, 86, 97, 109, 110
victimhood 112
violence xii, xiii, 8, 9, 39, 40, 45, 46,
  57, 83, 101, 111, 112
virgin 105, 109, 111

W

western v, vi, vii, ix, xv, xxii, xxiii, 3,
  5, 6, 11, 12, 14, 15, 20, 21, 22, 27,
  28, 30, 31, 42, 45, 47, 48, 50, 81,
  82, 83, 84, 86, 87, 88, 91, 93, 94,
  95, 97, 104, 112
wonder 3, 8, 25, 26, 33
worldview xi, 12, 22, 27, 29, 82, 85,
  87, 93, 94

Z

zenanas 99
Zoroastrianism 57

www.ingramcontent.com/pod-product-compliance
Lightning Source LLC
Chambersburg PA
CBHW070838020526
44114CB00041B/1953